Coventry and Warwickshire 1914-1919

Local Aspects of the Great War

(Volume 1)

Edited by Chris Holland

ᏣᏰ

2012

Warwickshire Great War Publications

Cover design by Warwick Printing

Published by:
Warwickshire Great War Publications
Plott Bungalow, Plott Lane, Stretton on Dunsmore, Nr Rugby CV23 9HR, UK
Tel: +44 (0)2476 542493
Email: poors_plot@tiscali.co.uk

ISBN: 978-0-9574216-1-5

A CIP catalogue record for this book is available from the British Library

Printed and bound by:
Warwick Printing, Caswell Rd, Leamington Spa, Warwickshire, CV31 1QD

Contents

ꞷ

Contributors

Gill Ashley-Smith has been involved with local history for more that 20 years, first in her home village of Kineton, and later in the county as a whole. In 2012 she and her husband, Peter, together received a joint award for their achievement in Local History from the British Association for Local History.

Janet Courtney has had a keen interest in local history for many years and was an active member of the Rugby Local History Research Group. Her original article concerning Belgian Refugees in Rugby was written for one of their 'Aspects' series of booklets about Rugby during the First World War.

Jeromy Hassell: like so many others, started to research his family history after his retirement. This has developed into a wider interest in history, and a few published articles as well as a series of talks have followed.

Chris Holland is a former head of History at King Henry VIII School, Coventry, and a recent branch chairman in the Western Front Association. His research, publications and talks reflect long-standing interests in local history and in the Great War.

Janet Leith was born in Coventry and attended a local grammar school. After raising a family, she worked for many years in various administrative posts with Coventry Education Department. In recent years her main interests have been in local and family history. She is a member of the Whitley Local History Group in Coventry.

James Sambrook, Emeritus Professor of English at the University of Southampton, is the author or editor of over a dozen books on eighteenth and nineteenth century literature, as well as the author of 'With the Rank and Pay of a Sapper', the history of the 216th (Nuneaton) Army Troops Company, Royal Engineers, in the Great War.

Philip Spinks was born in Stratford-upon-Avon and continues to live there; he is married with one son. After service in the Royal Artillery and the Sultan of Oman's Artillery he followed a second career as an ambulance paramedic. Now retired, he researches and writes on various aspects of local history and is a volunteer at the Shakespeare Centre Library and Archive.

Susan Tall is a family and local historian with an MA in Victorian Studies awarded by Leicester University. Her interest in the Great War arose from research into those commemorated on Kenilworth war memorial. She wrote the book "Kenilworth and the Great War" with Betty Sunley and has a website: www.kenilworth-war-memorial.org.uk . Sue gives talks on local history and is a volunteer at Warwickshire County Record Office.

Acknowledgements

First, and most obviously, I would like to thank my fellow contributors for the time, effort and support they have given to the project. Their research, knowledge and expertise are extensive and greatly appreciated. No study of local aspects of the Great War in the Coventry and Warwickshire area would be possible without the resources made available by the Coventry History Centre, the Warwickshire County Record Office, the Shakespeare Birthplace Trust, the Warwickshire Library Service and the Coventry History Centre and its predecessors and I would like to express the appreciation of all the contributors for the help of the permanent staff and volunteers of those institutions.

Many other people have contributed to this study, in a variety of ways, but I would like to thank a number in particular. Bob Bearman, Editor of the Journal of the Warwickshire Local History Society, kindly raised no objection to the use of two articles which had previously appeared in the Journal, and which make up Chapters 8 and 9. Peter Huxford has been, as always, an invaluable source of advice, comment and encouragement. I am also indebted to Chris Baker, who checked the Introduction, and to Diane Holland, who proof-read the text. I list the sources of illustrations used below but I would particularly like to thank David Fry for kindly offering material from his extensive photo-archive collection. Chris Tompsett generously allowed access to his own research into the period; moreover, it was as a result of conversations with Chris that the idea first arose of trying to bring together, in book form, research on the impact of the Great War on Coventry and Warwickshire.

Illustrations:
Other than those held by the contributors, the illustrations have been kindly provided courtesy of:

- The Warwickshire County Record Office: No. 2 (PH 815/21/5) 3 (PH 352/196/46) 29 (PH 352/91/108) 30 (PH 350/1911);
- Rugby Library: No. 12 (T 940.4.8);
- The Shakespeare Birthplace Trust: No. 18 (SC42/1705);
- Coventry Central Library and Coventry Archives (now Coventry History Centre): No. 22 and 23; maps Ch. 6;
- David Fry: No. 1, 13 and 16;
- Jerry Ash: No. 14;
- Peggy Bloom: No. 6;
- Chilvers Coton Heritage Centre: No. 9 and 10;
- Stoneleigh Abbey Preservation Trust: No. 25;
- David Beaumont: No. 21.

Introduction

ᘓ

No doubt it is still the case that "War makes rattling good history"[1] and the Great War, in particular, continues to exercise a remarkable hold on the British imagination. A body of research that is already considerable will be significantly increased by the end of the war's centenary. This reflects the continued fascination with the war's terrible cost, its pivotal role in shaping the twentieth century and its almost limitless human stories and tragedies. At one end of the spectrum, it appeals to those captivated by the clash of nations, at the other, to those absorbed in family history. Local historians sit somewhere in between.

In the Coventry and Warwickshire area, as elsewhere, there are a growing number of publications about those commemorated on local memorials. These studies provide an appropriate reminder of the enormous sacrifices that many families and communities made in the Great War and offer some guarantee that those commemorated will not be forgotten – that 'we will remember them'. In some cases, such work is part of a wider consideration of the war's impact on a particular community – a town, village or school, for example – and some of the contributors to this book have been involved in this way.[2] To look at the war's impact at a county level is comparatively unusual[3] but it has certain advantages. It enables some of the finer detail, so important in showing the impact of the war on individuals and their communities, to be combined with an overview, which illustrates the more general themes of that period and can sometimes challenge commonly-held interpretations of events. This collection of essays takes some of those themes – such as recruitment, treatment of the wounded, the impact on industry and agriculture – and illustrates them at a level that is sufficiently local to allow for examples that are specific. Other chapters focus on the impact across the area of events such as the outbreak of the war or the 'Spanish' 'flu but, again, do not lose sight of that detail.

It has to be said that the definition of 'Coventry and Warwickshire' that has been employed is somewhat arbitrary, as more recent boundary changes have altered the Warwickshire of the early twentieth century. Birmingham is not included in this study: a city that large and important deserves separate consideration. However, Coventry has been rescued from its exile to the West Midlands and reunited with the county of which it was a vital component. Even without Birmingham, the area at the time of the Great War was rich in diversity: agricultural areas and market towns (and a spa town) were juxtaposed with coal mining and other extractive industries, as well as with major centres of industrial production, containing engineering firms that were among the most technologically advanced in the country.

~

As Sellar and Yeatman remind us, "History is not what you thought. *It is what you can remember.*"[4] Our national memory of the Great War does not always stand up to scrutiny and that certainly seems to be true of the response to the outbreak of war, at least in the

Coventry and Warwickshire area **(Chapter 1)**. That it was a time of heightened national consciousness is not in question, although contemporaries were quick to point out the contrast with the public mood during the Boer War of 1899-1902 and to praise local people for their restrained behaviour at the outbreak of this new war on 4th August, 1914. Departing troops were afforded a rousing send off, even if their initial destinations were no more dangerous than Weymouth, but the local pace of recruitment for the New Army was initially steady rather than spectacular, and the rush to enlist only really got under way at the very end of August. Confidence in the justice of the Allied cause was accompanied by apprehension as to the impact that the war might have. Panic buying of food-stuffs was short-lived but concerns remained as to the dislocating effects of hostilities on the local economy. Those who urged "business as usual" did so more in the hope that this would reduce disruption than to demonstrate the phlegmatic qualities of the nation. Kitchener's appeal for a New Army would have caused any who thought the war might soon be over to reconsider and the generous and speedy response to relief funds also suggests that many did not expect the war to be short or easy. The phrase 'over by Christmas' seems conspicuous by its absence both in August and in the months that followed, at least at a local level. The often jaunty and confident tone of soldiers' letters published in the newspapers does not seem to have been widely reciprocated among the civilian population. What there was, however, was an intense and widespread desire to do something practical to aid the country in its time of crisis, and the outbreak of war was followed by a considerable, if sometimes misdirected, burst of energy.

In particular, the arrival of Belgian refugees in the area, in the autumn of 1914, triggered a remarkable response. A potent symbol of one of the main causes for which it was believed the war was being fought, the plight of the refugees touched many. It also provided an early opportunity for local people to make a practical contribution and to see the effects of their efforts at close hand. The analysis by Janet Leith, Janet Courtney and Susan Tall of the Belgian refugees in Coventry, Rugby and Kenilworth **(Chapter 2)** also illustrates what was happening in many communities in the area and, indeed, in the country as a whole. The speed with which committees were established, properties made available and furnished, garments produced and relief funds set up testifies not just to local goodwill, a sense of duty and considerable organisational powers, but also to the enormous energy that was unlocked by the arrival of the refugees. It is hard to know quite what the refugees made of the reception parties at local railway stations, often led by civic dignitaries, or of the crowds of visitors who came to inspect them in their new homes, but they can have been left in little doubt as to the warmth of local feeling. Newspapers in the early months of the war were full of articles about "our Belgian guests", of their experiences at the hands of the enemy and of the attempts being made to make them feel at home, in accordance, of course, with their social status. By contrast, local newspapers in the middle and later stages of the war have relatively little to say about the refugees. In part, this reflects the increasing integration of the refugees into the local communities, as many found jobs and were able to support their families. However, it also reflects the other demands that the war was making on people's time, finances and goodwill. Inevitably, the plight of the Belgian refugees was surpassed by the losses that British communities were suffering as a result of the ever-lengthening casualty lists in the war.

Although more than two million Britons volunteered for the armed forces in the first 17 months of the war, recruitment was never as straightforward as the authorities wished. As noted, the rush to enlist only really began in Coventry and Warwickshire at the very end of August 1914 and it generally did not last long. The area produced no 'pals' battalion, although the idea was briefly mooted for Rugby, but local pride was reflected in the pre-war Territorials, notably the 7th Battalion of the Royal Warwickshire Regiment and the Warwickshire Yeomanry, and in the subsequent recruitment of their reserves.

It was also seen in the raising of other units with local associations, such as the 216th Fortress Company of the Royal Engineers. In turn, the growing need for engineering units reflects the way in which the war soon changed on the Western Front, with the onset of static, trench warfare. The '216' was recruited in Nuneaton and there was a determination to fill all places in the Company with local men. It was also initially clothed, fed, paid for and housed by the town. Jim Sambrook's account **(Chapter 3)** of the raising of the Company is informed by the memories of some of those who joined up and provides a full and sympathetic account of how the unit was put together, of its early training and experiences, and of the backgrounds of many of those involved. There can be few British units raised in the volunteer stage of recruitment about whom such an insight exists.

High among local concerns in the early stages of the war were the economic consequences of the exodus of large numbers of young men into the armed forces. These included the loss of income to families, reduced expenditure in shops and amenities, and the loss of rent generated by lodgers. The arrival of the 29th Division in the area, in the early months of 1915, was therefore regarded by most as a welcome boost to the local economy, even if it initially brought concerns as to the behaviour of so many unknown soldiers. The billeting of regular army soldiers on the civilian community was unusual, in that most were being sent as quickly as possible to the Western Front, and resulted from the need to turn a collection of battalions that had been serving in the Empire into a fighting division. It was an event that had an impact on the area out of all proportion to the relatively short time that the 29th Division was there. The experiences of Rugby **(Chapter 4)** have been chosen to represent those of local communities upon whom soldiers were billeted. Local links with the 29th Division were to last well beyond its departure for Gallipoli, and find permanent expression in the monument near Stretton on Dunsmore. The inscription records not only the subsequent exploits of the 'Immortal' 29th Division but also the fact that the Division stayed in the area; indeed, the idea for a memorial to the Division was being suggested even before the 29th landed at Gallipoli in April 1915.

During the Great War, the soldiers of Britain, her dominions and colonies suffered more than two million non-fatal wounds. Many of the wounded did not need evacuation from the theatre of war but others were sent to Britain for treatment and convalescence. Prominent among the hospitals that received these casualties were those run by Voluntary Aid Detachments. Part of the pre-war Territorial Force, VADs became an important aspect of the local war effort and by 1917 they were responsible for the running of 35 hospitals in Warwickshire alone. One of the earliest and most important of these was the VAD hospital in Kineton, and its development and success are traced by Gillian Ashley-Smith **(Chapter 5)**. The chapter provides more than just a revealing insight into the running of a hospital that, by the war's end, had treated well over 2,000 patients. It also reflects the way in which the Government increasingly harnessed voluntary effort during the war and the strict standards to which volunteers, many no more than girls, were held. It shows the way in which a hospital could become a focal point for a local community, with villagers not just involved in the running of the hospital but in fund-raising activities and in entertainments for the wounded soldiers. The Clarendon House hospital at Kineton was clearly a source of local pride, and the hospital's only fatality a matter of shared regret. Moreover, the chapter also illustrates the importance that pre-war social leaders frequently retained during the conflict, especially in rural areas, and their often considerable organisational powers and tenacity of purpose. If social status bestowed privilege, then it also entailed obligations that were invariably taken seriously.

Increasingly, the war became what the Germans called a *Materialschlacht*, a battle to produce the armaments that would crush the enemy and economise on the lives of your soldiers. It was inevitable that Coventry would play a major role in this struggle. Its rapid industrial expansion before the war meant that it possessed light engineering factories producing a wide range of goods, including bicycles, motorcycles and motor vehicles, as well as their components, along with machine tools and artificial silk. The city's population had risen from 46,000 in 1881 to 106,000 in 1911, reflecting not just boundary changes but migration from other parts of the country. In the words of Kenneth Richardson: "By the time the First World War began, a greatly increased population, which had been organised into large productive units in peace, could easily be transferred to production in war."[7] Jeromy Hassell's study of White & Poppe Ltd **(Chapter 6)** is an excellent example of the rapid expansion of Coventry's industry during the war and the massive contribution that it made to the national war effort. The figures for the workforce alone are remarkable: starting with 350 in August 1914, White and Poppe, during the course of the war, would employ more than 30,000 people. By the end of the war, the firm was running one of the largest munitions works in the country, with production spread across three major factories. Moreover, the speed with which expansion took place questions the assumption that it was only in the middle and later stages of the war that Britain began to gear up its industrial production. The success of White & Poppe mirrors that of other firms in the city, such as Daimler, Standard, Rover, Siddeley-Deasy, Triumph, Courtaulds and Alfred Herbert's, as well, of course, as the Ordnance Works. As Jeromy Hassell's account shows, such expansion would not have been possible without the large scale employment of female workers, as well as a significant level of migration from other parts of the country, which caused the city's population to increase still further, to 136,000 by 1919. Overcrowding was one of the resultant problems in Coventry and long working hours and the 'dilution of labour' caused industrial relations to become strained. Nonetheless, the abiding impression is of the city's wartime dynamism and purpose.

Agriculture was also involved in a battle for production. Britain was heavily dependent upon food imports and, in 1914, could only feed its population for 125 days in the year, from its own produce. Although the harvest for 1914 went well, the problems caused by the loss of agricultural labourers to the Army, the requisitioning of many farm horses and the impact of German submarines were causing increasing concern in 1915. Susan Tall's account of food production and control in the Kenilworth area **(Chapter 7)** carefully traces the often complex process by which food production was increased, not only on farms but on allotments, and even by the gathering of wild fruit from the countryside. This increase was accompanied by measures to make the most of what food was grown and, increasingly, to ensure its fair distribution. The whole process was marked by tensions and conflicts of interest. Farmers' determination to retain skilled labour – often including members of their own families – was at odds with the Army's increasing demands for fresh recruits. Alternative labour was not easy to find. Farmers were often suspicious of female labour and many local women understandably preferred to find better-paid employment in munitions factories. Soldiers released by the Army to help farmers, or discharged from the Army as a result of injury, often lacked the necessary skills. The same was true of German prisoners of war, who were not, in any case, released in large numbers until 1918. Many local education authorities, including Warwickshire's, were reluctant to release children prematurely from education, which would reverse the progress of the pre-war period. Rising prices were an incentive to farmers to plough up more land but increasingly led to demands to control inflation and thereby reduce wage claims. Nonetheless, by the end of the war, nearly 3 million extra acres of land had been ploughed up, much of it in the Midlands, and Britain could feed its population for 155 days.[8] If the increase seems modest by comparison with some of the prodigious feats of productivity in industry, Britain was the only European belligerent to increase food production during the war.[9] Food rationing and economies meant the British civilian population often made do with less, but they remained reasonably fed by comparison with Germany, whose people had been reduced to a wretched state by 1918 by the effects of war.

Heavy losses in the fighting and the competing demands on the male population made by the Army and by the economy meant that Britain faced an increasingly serious manpower shortage. There are few better examples to illustrate these conflicting needs, and the tensions that resulted from them, than the work of the 'war courts' – the tribunals whose job it was to consider claims for exemption from military service. As Philip Spinks explains, Warwickshire is fortunate in that more information has survived on the working of the appeals system than in most parts of the country and, in **Chapter 8**, he considers the work of the Stratford-upon-Avon Borough Tribunal. The tribunals were initially set up in 1915, under the Derby Scheme, to consider the appeals of men who had attested their willingness to serve but who believed that they had special grounds for delay. Following the introduction of conscription in 1916, the tribunals were used to deal with those who sought exemption from military service. The tribunals have not always had a good press, especially when it came to dealing with those whose appeal was based on the grounds of conscience: "they might prove uncomprehending in response and arbitrary in decision – not to say sometimes downright cruel".[10] In fact, as Philip Spinks shows, less than 1% of the claims coming before the Stratford Borough Tribunal were to do with conscientious objection, by comparison with more than 43% of claims that were lodged by employers seeking to retain labour or delay the loss of such labour. Although a tribunal contained a military representative, his role was advisory and the tribunal's membership was essentially civilian. The Stratford Borough Tribunal clearly tried to be even-handed in dealing with cases that often defied easy solution and they proved rather more lenient than might be expected. Members did their best to reconcile the needs of the nation with those of their own district. Perhaps the Stratford Borough Tribunal was atypical, although a not dissimilar picture has emerged for Kineton, which was served by the Stratford Rural District Tribunal.[11]

'Spanish' influenza, the contemporary name for the influenza pandemic caused by the H1N1 virus, was a natural event, although one whose spread was influenced by the war, notably through the movement of troops. Nonetheless, the impact of the 'flu in the later stages of the war and in the early post-war period added considerably to the misery that war had caused. Although it is tempting to assume that its depredations fell more heavily on a British society that was suffering increasing hardship after some four years of war, this was not necessarily the case. Societies unaffected by war or where the civilian population were not subject to privation, as was the case in the United States, proved just as susceptible to the impact of the 'flu. However, the war did make it harder for British society to cope with the effects of the 'flu, with more than half the country's doctors, as well as many of its nurses, serving overseas. Fuel restrictions meant houses were colder and public transport more crowded. The absence in the forces of so many men put added burdens on women, many of whom had taken wartime jobs. Local authorities, already stretched by the demands of war, and conscious of the need to maintain wartime production, were faced with a pandemic they had no means of halting. The considerable number of fatalities caused by the 'flu, including an estimated 2,500 in Coventry and Warwickshire, came on top of those losses suffered in the fighting. **Chapter 9** traces the arrival of the Spanish 'flu in Britain and its effect on the local area.

The signing of the Armistice in 1918 coincided with the height of 'Spanish' influenza in the area and that was one reason why the local response to news of the Armistice, the subject of **Chapter 10**, was perhaps surprisingly muted. Clearly there was considerable satisfaction that a great victory had been won and many saw this triumph as vindication of the causes for which it was believed the war had been fought. However, there was also an awareness of the obvious human cost of that victory, coupled with uncertainty as to what the future would hold, especially for those employed in industries that had grown with the war and were dependent upon Government contracts. For the most part, however there was simply relief that the war was over and that an end was now in sight to the anxieties and hardships of wartime. The accounts of how local people celebrated the news – largely a mixture of religious devotion and good-humoured merriment – seem a long way from the almost riotous scenes in London, which have tended to influence our ideas of Armistice Day in 1918. As one Coventry paper put it: "Coventry rejoiced but quietly. ... After four terrible years it is no wonder that many people have lost the ability to spontaneously rise to a condition of gaiety."[12] It was also far removed from the disturbances in Coventry that came after the Peace Celebrations in July 1919, when three nights of rioting reflected the tensions that had built up in the city during the war, as well as the social and economic problems that emerged in Britain after the Armistice.

~

Finally, this consideration of local aspects of the Great War is entitled 'Volume 1'. There is already material, either completed or in the process of completion, that will go towards Volume 2. However, there remain a number of important topics that are not yet covered – such as the effect of the war on local education or on industrial relations in the area. It is to be hoped, therefore, that this initial study might encourage others to contribute their own research and, in turn, develop further our understanding of the Great War's impact on Coventry and Warwickshire.

Chris Holland

Stretton on Dunsmore, November 2012

---

1 Thomas Hardy: *The Dynasts,* 1904. ("War makes rattling good history; but Peace is poor reading.")

2 See, in particular, Gillian Ashley-Smith: *Kineton in the Great War, 1914-21,* Brewin Books, 1999; Susan Tall (with Betty Sunley): *Kenilworth and the Great War: A Tribute to the Fallen;* Clock Tower Publications, 2004 and Chris Holland (with Rob Phillips): *Doing Its Part Nobly: Coventry's King Henry VIII School and the Great War;* Plott Green Publications, 2005.

3 However, Keith Grieves: *Sussex in the First World War;* The Sussex Record Society, Lewes, 2000, provides a comprehensive study at the county level.

4 W.C. Sellar and R.J. Yeatman: *1066 And All That;* Methuen 1930.

5 See also Stuart Halifax: *Over by Christmas: British popular opinion and the short war in 1914;* First World War Studies, 1:2, 2010.

6 *Statistics Of The Military Effort Of The British Empire During The Great War 1914-1920;* Part IV, Casualties, Table (i) (a); War Office 1922.

7 Kenneth Richardson: *Twentieth Century Coventry;* City of Coventry, 1972.

8 Pamela Horn: *Rural Life in England in the First World War;* Dublin 1984.

9 Caroline Dakers: *The Countryside at War 1914-18;* Constable 1987.

10 Trevor Wilson: *The Myriad Faces of War: Britain and the Great War, 1914-1918;* Polity Press, Cambridge, 1988.

11 Peter Ashley-Smith: *Kineton and the Military Tribunals, 1915-1918;* Warwickshire History, Summer 2005.

12 *Coventry Herald:* November 15th-16th, 1918.

Chapter 1

The Outbreak of War

The response in Coventry and Warwickshire, August 1914

Chris Holland

☙

It has been said of Britain in 1914 that: "war was widely expected as an eventual probability, but it was scarcely visualised as an immediate contingency".[1] The underlying tensions in Europe, most obviously the Anglo-German naval race, were sufficiently familiar that the *Leamington Spa Courier* could state, on 7th August, that: "we are now at the beginning of that great European war which has been the dread of thoughtful men for so long". However, the developments of the summer of 1914 largely unfolded without holding popular attention. The assassination of Franz Ferdinand, on 28th June, was, of course, reported in the British press but neither the event nor its immediate aftermath were attributed the significance they deserved and the crisis in Ireland continued to dominate the headlines of the national newspapers. It was not until the end of July that there was a growing recognition that Britain might become involved in a European war, a likelihood that grew very much greater when Germany declared war on Russia on 1st August.

In Coventry, journalist Henry Wilkins started his "Journal of the Great European War" with an entry for 1st August, which began: "The shadows deepened, the streets were filled with people desirous of learning the news." On a personal level, he worried for the safety of his daughter, Nan, who had been in Belgium since the preceding Sunday.[2] Coventry's Mayor, Siegfried Bettmann, of German birth but a naturalised Briton, had a keener understanding than most of what was at stake. The founder of the Triumph Company, he was asked by the War Office to convene a meeting of motor cycle manufacturers before the outbreak of war. When told, in confidence, that the motor cycles were intended for use in Belgium, Bettmann "knew that the fate of Europe was sealed".[3] At Stoneleigh Abbey, Cordelia Leigh noted that the Stoneleigh village Post Office had to be kept open day and night on Sunday (2nd August) for possible telephone messages – "a small local incident which seemed to bring matters home very closely to us".[4] The same day, the Vicar of Holy Trinity Church, in Coventry, the Rev. R.B. Littlewood, warned that "God intended to chastise Europe for her sins"; the service was accompanied, somewhat melodramatically, by two loud crashes, at 11.45 a.m. and 12.15 p.m., which proved to be pieces of stone that had fallen from the tower onto the roof of the organ chamber.[5] On 3rd August, Germany declared war on France and Henry Wilkins wrote gloomily: "The die is cast ... The great catastrophe has come upon Europe." The following day, the news came that the German Army had invaded Belgium and Asquith gave his ultimatum to Germany to withdraw her troops by 11 p.m. (midnight in Berlin). With the passing of that deadline, Britain declared war on Germany and was drawn into what the *Rugby Advertiser* soon described as "The Great Continental War".[6]

The rapidly deteriorating situation in Europe did not discourage the local exodus on the August Bank Holiday weekend. Indeed, it may have encouraged it, as people sought to take their pleasure whilst they could. In Coventry, the rush started on the Friday, 31st July, and, by the end of Saturday, an estimated 25,000 people had left the city by train, with the favourite destinations being Blackpool, North Wales, Bournemouth, Hastings, Bexhill, Eastbourne, London, Ireland and Scotland. These record numbers were partly explained by the clubs, provided by local firms, into which employees paid money, subsequently withdrawn for annual holidays. The development was welcomed by the *Coventry Herald*, which noted approvingly that "the artisan class" was now taking annual holidays, instead of "wandering the streets".[7] However, many Coventrians who delayed their excursions until the Monday missed out. Although the early excursions ran, the rest were cancelled as the needs of the Army assumed priority. Holiday makers from Rugby fared better: practically all Bank Holiday excursions were run.

The situation in Europe became the absorbing topic of conversation. The *Coventry Herald* noted that: "the disappointment at spoilt holidays was submerged into the greater concern for the country's welfare".[8] On Tuesday, in Leamington, Cordelia Leigh noticed "little boys marching solemnly along after a miniature Union Jack, armed with sticks and toy guns".[9] News that war had been declared reached Coventry about midnight on Tuesday. There were still plenty of people about in the centre of the town "and the effect on them was inspiring". There was great cheering for several minutes, followed by the spontaneous singing of 'Rule Britannia' and 'Three Cheers for the Red, White and Blue'. The effect was heightened by the display of the Union Jack. The arrival of Territorial soldiers on a night march from Nuneaton (see below) almost synchronised with the procession that had formed and was moving in the direction of the Drill Hall. The appearance of the Nuneaton men "added enthusiasm". It was "a night to be remembered" and the culmination of "an amazing Bank holiday".[10]

Even before the outbreak of war, preparations were being made to implement the initial, precautionary, phase of mobilisation. The 4th (Extra Reserve) Battalion of the Royal Warwickshire Regiment had returned to Warwick on Saturday (1st August) from the Isle of Wight, where it had been involved in its annual training. On arrival at Budbrooke Barracks, west of Warwick, the Battalion received orders to return to the Isle of Wight immediately, by a specially chartered train. The men received an enthusiastic send off. The 3rd and 4th Battalions of the Royal Warwickshire Regiment were part of the Special Reserve, made up of men who had undertaken six months training before returning to civilian life. They had enlisted for six years and had agreed to further annual training (of three to four weeks) and to be ready to be called up in the event of a general mobilisation. The Regiment's 3rd (Reserve) Battalion subsequently arrived at Budbrooke on Wednesday (5th August), before leaving on Saturday (8th August). It was the particular task of the Reserve battalions to protect the country's ports.

Soldiers of the regular army remained on the Army Reserve following their period of full time service with the colours. Their commitment was typically seven years with the colours and five years on the Reserve (for the infantry; other arms had slightly different arrangements). The Reservists were essential to bring up to strength the battalions that would make up the original British Expeditionary Force (BEF). The King signed the proclamation to mobilise the armed forces at 11 a.m. on 4th August, with War Office orders being sent out at 4.40 p.m. Reservists were informed of mobilisation by telegram, although posters were also displayed, and they had to report immediately to their regimental depots. Here, they were given a medical inspection and issued with kit, before being despatched to their units. The reporting of the Reservists to their depots took place quickly. In Coventry, more than 700 (including Navy Reservists) left in the space of 24 hours, and the total by the 7th August was about 1,000. Each would already have been issued with a railway warrant but processing these still put a heavy demand on railway clerical staff. The Post Offices also found themselves with a heavy workload dealing with telegrams. Taking place quickly, and not in organised groups, the departure of the Army Reservists appears to have been less of a focus for popular emotions than the movements of the Territorials, beyond, of course, the immediate families of the Reservists. Indeed, it was the departure of the Territorials from Coventry on Wednesday evening (August 5th) that was described by the *Coventry Herald* as "the greatest event of this sensational week".[11]

On Bank Holiday Saturday (1st August), the Territorial Force (TF) soldiers who made up the 7th Battalion of the Royal Warwickshire Regiment, in turn part of the Warwickshire Infantry Brigade, had left for Rhyl to take part in the annual camp. Despite the deepening crisis in Europe, the Government initially agreed to allow the TF summer camps to go ahead, fearing that to cancel them "would indicate too clearly that Britain was preparing for a war that it still hoped to avert".[12] However, on 2nd August, Asquith was persuaded to recall the TF. Not to do so would delay mobilisation by tying up trains needed for the movement of troops; it would also delay the deployment of the TF to their home defence stations. Accordingly, all TF camps were cancelled by the War Office and the troops of the Warwickshire Brigade, like others, were sent home to await further instructions. The local men arrived back in their home towns during the course of Monday afternoon, 3rd August. At 7 p.m. the same evening, orders were received to 'embody' (unite) the TF, with concentration taking place on Coventry. Full mobilisation followed on the afternoon of Tuesday, 4th August. In Coventry, notices were posted throughout the city instructing members of the 7th Battalion to proceed to headquarters. During Tuesday evening, men in full equipment began arriving at the Drill Hall, usually accompanied by relatives and friends, many of whom remained outside the Hall. Some "youthful spirits" among the men lowered a rope by which refreshments were raised, this being the cause of "a good deal of merriment".[13] The men spent the night at the Hall, a cart with groceries arriving at 2 a.m. In Rugby, the 'Terriers' also assembled at their Drill Hall on Tuesday. They were given a hasty medical examination, before the first contingent (about 100) travelled to the station to take the 11.05 p.m. train to Coventry; the second contingent (about 40) went on the 2.00 a.m. train. An enormous crowd assembled outside the Drill Hall to see the men start and accompanied them to the railway station. The down platform at Rugby was "thronged". Mr J.J. McKinnell, Chairman of the Council, and other members of the Council were present, Mr McKinnell making a short speech. "Tremendous cheering" accompanied the departure of the first train.

In Nuneaton, the local Company[14] arrived at their Drill Hall, in full marching kit, between 7 and 8 p.m. on Tuesday. Many men were accompanied by families and girlfriends and a huge crowd assembled in the vicinity of the Recreation Ground. By 9 p.m. the adjacent roads were almost impassable. A medical inspection was conducted shortly before 10 p.m., followed by a prayer by the Rev. Bedale, after which the Company marched out 120 strong, led by Capt. J.M. Knox. As they stepped into Pool Bank Street, a "terrific cheer went up". Their journey to Coventry was to be on foot. The men received "another fine reception" as they marched through Bedworth, despite the lateness of the hour. Headquarters in Coventry were reached "in good time". The offer by the Nuneaton Borough Band to play the men from the town was declined by Knox, as he felt the matter was "too serious for a parade".[15] In Leamington, 'F' Company reported at the Drill Hall in Adelaide Road at 11 pm. on Tuesday. A medical examination led to 5 men being rejected; the remainder then left at 12.20 a.m. on Wednesday morning to begin their 10 mile march to Coventry, as a train could not be found to take them there. 'G' Company (Warwick) also made a night march to Coventry, passing through Kenilworth at 3 a.m., two hours after the Leamington men. On arrival in Coventry, the outstation companies were lodged overnight in the Grammar School (King Henry VIII School).

The departure from Coventry of the newly assembled 7th Battalion took place on Wednesday evening, 5th August. However, it was rumoured that they would leave on Wednesday morning and many people came down to the Drill Hall. By the time the Battalion did depart, at 7 p.m., an immense crowd had gathered along the route to the station. A band headed the procession and played 'Auld Lang Syne' as the soldiers marched into the station's private entrance, at the end of the station yard. Although the public were excluded from the station platform, several thousand gathered within the station precincts. The first train left at 7.28 p.m. for Swindon, the second shortly after. From Swindon, the troops then travelled on to Weymouth, as part of the plan to guard the South coast. The *Rugby Advertiser* commented that there was no surprise that Weymouth was the destination for the Territorials, "it having been understood for some years that Weymouth would be the Warwickshire Brigade's depot in the event of war".[16] In fact their stay there was brief, the Brigade being brought back almost immediately to the Swindon area, before moving on to Chelmsford.

The other local Territorial Force units were also being brought together, although their departure from the area took place a few days after that of the Infantry. The 4th South Midland (Howitzer) Brigade, Royal Field Artillery (RFA), had two local batteries: the 4th, based in Coventry and the 5th, based in Rugby. On Saturday, 1st August, the Batteries had left for annual training at Lydd, in Kent, arriving there in the early hours of Sunday. They were recalled on Monday. At Rugby, Mrs Nickalls, wife of Capt. Nickalls, got a "good tea" ready for the men when they arrived at the Drill Hall. The 'Howitzers' were allowed seven days from the Wednesday to mobilise. The Rugby Battery was kept together after its return from camp – the headquarters being used for meals and sleeping purposes and the horses located in the field opposite. The men were kept busy cleaning, exercising and drilling. Those not on duty were given leave to go into town. In Coventry, the men from the 4th Battery spent seven days at the Drill Hall, before departing for Swindon on Tuesday, 11th August. The advance party left at 2 a.m.; the main party followed during the day, their departure watched by another large crowd of well-wishers.

The Warwickshire Yeomanry and the Warwickshire Royal Horse Artillery (RHA) had already held their annual training: their membership was generally drawn from the more rural sectors of society and training was held in advance of the harvest period. During the first week of the war, the Yeomanry received notices of embodiment and began to assemble at their regimental headquarters, at St John's, in Warwick, on the afternoon of Wednesday (5th August). Their departure from their localities was accompanied by scenes similar to those already noted. At Shipston-on-Stour, for example, "the biggest crowd that has ever been seen at the railway station" gathered the see the men leave, along with several Reservists. The National Anthem was played and a large Union Jack was fastened to the front of the train's engine.[17] At Warwick, the Yeomanry were billeted locally, with an allowance paid of 2s per man, per day, for messing and a bed; stabling for horses was at the rate of 1s 9d per horse, per day. The following week, the Warwickshire Yeomanry were joined in Warwick by the Worcestershire Yeomanry and the Gloucestershire Yeomanry, as well as by the Army Service Corps and the Ambulance Corps of the South Midlands Brigade. The town was full of men in uniform and the commons of St Mary's and St Nicholas's had

hope was expressed that there would soon be "a large army of local women" who would be making articles for "our brave men on the field of battle". Regulation patterns were available and financial donations were invited.

The instinct 'to do something' was not restricted to women. In Rugby, at the meeting of the UDC, on Wednesday, 5th August, the proposal was made to create a body of men "of good physique" to meet "patriotic needs".[29] This led to the formation of the Rugby Patriotic Association, which quickly enrolled some 700 men. Drilling began and guards were soon stationed at Mill Road tunnel, under the railway station. It was anticipated that members of the Association could replace men removed from the police, fire brigade, ambulance service etc, as well helping with the harvest. Colonel Malcolm Little acted as Chairman. The Association was initially undeterred by the Government's opposition to local forces and about 500 of its members drilled on the Lower School (Lawrence Sheriff) field each evening. Reluctantly, however, drilling was suspended in response to War Office pressure, although the intention was expressed that the organisation should be retained.

In Coventry, a meeting was held on Wednesday, 12th August, at the Out Patients Department of Coventry and Warwickshire Hospital, to consider the formation of a local defence force. The initiative was taken by a group of prominent citizens who included Alfred Herbert and Edward Iliffe, and the meeting was presided over by the Mayor. Herbert argued that a force could be useful for a variety of tasks, including scouting, despatch carrying, guarding railways, bridges and waterworks, ambulance work and conveying the wounded. Colonel Wyley promised military officers who would advise on matters such as drill. The force would also endeavour to encourage recruiting. The decision was taken to set up the Coventry Citizen's Defence Force; at a subsequent meeting, at the Drill Hall, Colonel Nutt took command. A company 120 strong, raised by Iliffe and Sons, soon began drilling. However, Government opposition led to the decision, on 24th August, not to proceed with the enrolment of a Defence Force in Coventry. Instead, magistrates were empowered to register a body of special constables whose duties covered some of the same objectives. Following a meeting on 17th August, a similar defence organisation was planned for Bedworth and Foleshill: the Citizens' League was intended to prepare every available man in the area in case of invasion, as well as undertaking the guarding of lines of communication. However, drilling did not start and the organisation never got beyond the planning stage. In Stratford-upon-Avon, a list had been quickly opened in the Town Hall, allowing people to register their names for service in any capacity; by 14th August, 350 men and 290 women had registered. About 250 men had joined the local rifle corps, their number including actors from the Memorial Theatre, who were drilling on a daily basis.

On 5th August, the Government passed the Aliens Restrictions Act and, by 8th August, Germans and Austrians over the age of 18 years began to register with the police. Their names were enrolled, photos were obtained and information recorded on occupations, places of business and residence, whether they had been in the service of a foreign government, and so forth. The penalty for non-compliance was a fine of up to £100 or imprisonment for up to 6 months; arrests could be made without a warrant. In the first few days, about 70 registered in Coventry, "most of whom were respectably dressed", according to the *Coventry Herald*.[30] All were interviewed by the Chief Constable. The great majority were German. Some had been living a long time in Coventry and had English wives; however, under English law, the wife and children of an alien took his nationality. In the event of Coventry being declared a 'prohibited area', aliens could only continue living in the city with a special permit. The same edition of the *Herald* also reported cases in Coventry of name plates being taken down from gates and house doors in order to prevent people with German sounding names from being subjected to unwanted attention.

Coventry's most famous 'alien' was, of course, its Mayor, Siegfried Bettmann. The founder of the Triumph Company had been born in Germany and, despite his distinguished contributions to the city, his position was difficult. Like other aliens, he was forced to register but, publicly, there was support for him. On 7th August, the *Coventry Herald* published an article by him on "The true cause of the War", in which he asked readers to distinguish between militaristic "Prussianism" and humanistic "Germanism". On 28th-29th August, the paper quoted a letter from *The Investor's Review*, which praised Bettmann, who was seen as an "enlightened German", and his considerable efforts on behalf of the city in the early weeks of the war also won approval. Privately, however, there were reservations about his position. On 13th August, Henry Wilkins noted in his Journal that: "His position is not an easy one. There are citizens who do not like the idea of a German being at the head of affairs at this time." Yet, only two days later, the War Office asked Triumph to provide 100 motor cycles – the first of more than 30,000 motor cycles that the company would eventually produce for the war effort. Bettmann himself recorded how "distrust crept into the minds of many" and, in September, he offered not to serve a second year as Mayor when his term of office came to an end in November. "The Council accepted his proposal with alacrity."[31]

In Rugby, on 11th August, a crowd of several hundred assembled in front of a second-hand clothing shop in Warwick Street, which was managed by a foreigner. It was rumoured that he was a German Jew and that he had been making uncomplimentary remarks about the King and his subjects. The man appeared at his door and was given "a hostile reception", until he was able to persuade the crowd that he and his wife were actually Russian Poles: he produced a photo of himself in the uniform of a Russian soldier. At this point, the crowd moved away, having sung "For he's a jolly good fellow". Someone else in Rugby who experienced a difficult time was a well-known J.P., Mr F. Merttens. In a letter to the *Rugby Advertiser* of 15th August, he pointed out that he had ceased to be a German subject in 1869 and was now British. He pleaded to be treated generously, "at the hands of a generous people". His support for the British cause was underlined two weeks later, when he gave his Minerva car, free of charge, to the Rugby Howitzer Battery. In Stratford-upon-Avon, Mr G. Chierici Kendall also found it necessary to write to the local newspaper to deny that he was German Jew and that he had been poisoning the local reservoir. He pointed out that his mother was English, his father Italian and that he had been born in Yorkshire. Nor had his son been arrested as a spy but was, in fact, on honeymoon in North Wales.[32]

Predictably, those who opposed the war were given little coverage in the press, and usually it was to report their weakness and unpopularity. Coventry's Liberal M.P., Mr D.M. Mason, was ridiculed for having suggested previously that that the Naval and Military Estimates should have been reduced and for having claimed that the idea of Germany attacking Britain was nonsense. The *Coventry Herald*, for 28th-29th August, reported that the Coventry Passive Resisters were a dwindling body, whose numbers had fallen from 70 or 80 to about 10. In Rugby, the *Advertiser* reported "disorderly scenes" in the Market Place on the night of Sunday, 9th August, when local Socialists tried to address a meeting in opposition to the war. Although listened to fairly patiently at first, the mood of the crowd changed and the police eventually had to intervene, escorting first one speaker and then a second away from the scene. The second speaker was followed by up to 500 people "jeering and singing". Showing considerable nerve, the first speaker then re-appeared, with the crowd transferring their attentions once more to him. He was finally taken off to the Police Station for his protection, in turn prompting the rumour that a German spy had been captured.[33] Two strangers carrying knapsacks who appeared at Long Itchington were soon rumoured to be spies and were unable to find accommodation for the night; the men – artists sketching in the area – had more success at Stockton.[34]

On 6th August, Parliament authorised an increase in the size of the Army by 500,000 men and the call for the first 100,000 appeared on 7th August. The *Rugby Advertiser* (15th

August) was one of the local papers containing the appeal 'Your King and Country Need You', although this was not yet accompanied by Kitchener's pointing finger. Those who wished to respond were invited to report to the Drill Hall by the newly appointed Recruiting Officer for the area, Colonel H.H. Mulliner. The same edition reported that 44 had so far enlisted in the town, with a dozen or so more due to be examined on Friday morning. The following Tuesday, 18th August, a recruiting meeting was held at the Skating Rink, with an attendance estimated at just under 5,000. Mr McKinnell presided but the main speech was given by Lord Denbigh, suitably dressed in khaki uniform. Colonel Mulliner was among other speakers, claiming that, in recruiting young men, he was doing them a good turn. Somewhat ambiguously, he argued that "in after-life" their wives and children would be proud that they had belonged to Kitchener's army. Music at the meeting was provided by the British Thomson-Houston (B.T.H.) band. By the 22nd, recruitment in Rugby had risen to 161, of whom 73 had been accepted on Thursday, 20th August, suggesting that the meeting had given a fillip to the process.

Recruiting in Coventry also proceeded steadily, with nearly 400 reported as having enlisted by 21st August. Between 50 and 60 had been rejected, "a comparatively low percentage", thought the *Coventry Herald*.[35] However, concerns were soon being expressed about the slow pace of recruitment in Nuneaton and a meeting was called in the town on 24th August, at the request of Colonel Mulliner. An estimated 3,000 men went to the Picturedrome in Leicester Road to listen to the Earl of Denbigh and others. (In total, the platform party comprised 22 local notables, including eight JPs and two MPs.) The Mayor of Nuneaton, Alderman W.T. Bates, said that he was sorry to say "that the numbers had not come up to expectations" – the 120 who had so far been recruited being insufficient for a district with a population of 40,000. One of the 120 who had already joined the colours in the Nuneaton district was George Gill. Summoned by his wife, Florence, for common assault, he had been due to appear at court the previous week. His absence was explained by his enlistment and the case was adjourned. It does at least suggest that not all of those who volunteered were motivated solely by patriotism.

On 4th August, the Government established a Cabinet Committee on the Prevention and Relief of Distress, and the Local Government Board (LGB) warned that the outbreak of war might involve considerable dislocation of trade, resulting in "a serious lack of employment in certain industries". The LGB suggested that, in towns of more than 20,000, distress committees should meet to consider schemes of work and stated that it would make grants to suitable schemes. It was proposed that committees should include not just representatives of the local authorities but also Boards of Guardians, Trade Unions and philanthropic societies.

Local authorities in the area were quick to respond. In fact, a Coventry Distress Committee already existed, created under the provisions of the 1905 Act of Parliament. It consisted of 25 members, including 12 members of the Council, but had hardly needed to meet in the years immediately before the war. On Friday, 7th August, a meeting of the Distress Committee led to the decision to create two General Committees: one to supplement the actions of the Distress Committee for those thrown out of work, the other to consider the opening of a Patriotic Fund to assist those suffering from the effects of the war. The same day, the Coventry Employers' Conference passed a resolution, proposed by Edward Iliffe and seconded by Alfred Herbert, urging local manufacturers to continue business on normal lines as far as possible and that any reduction of time worked should take the form of a reduced number of hours worked per day, for a five day week, rather than a reduction in the number of days. The Distress Committee in Coventry was soon giving consideration to works upon which the unemployed could be engaged during the crisis, such as levelling ground on Hearsall Common and the Radford Recreation Ground, or the construction of a new storage reservoir at Coundon. By the end of August, the LGB had sanctioned the building of 100 houses to accommodate tenants from Leicester Street, whose dwellings were due to be demolished as the thoroughfare was improved.

In Rugby, a special meeting of the UDC was held on 5th August to consider how emergencies arising from the war might be dealt with and to reassure the town's inhabitants that the Council was "determined to take all steps that might be necessary". The local Rector suggested the formation of a Committee for Relieving Distress among the families of local Reservists, although the scope of the assistance was soon widened to include the dependents of all those who were serving their country. On 10th August, a Council meeting led to the formation of a Local Distress Committee, whose members also included representatives of local firms. In Warwick, a meeting was convened by the Lord Lieutenant (the Earl of Craven) and the High Sheriff (Colonel Wyley) and held at the Shire Hall on 15th August, as the county responded to the LGB's initiative. It proposed the creation of a fund that would be used to support a variety of causes.

On 6th August, the Prince of Wales issued an appeal for a National Relief Fund and the response was immediate, even if it did sometimes cut across local funds that had been created. In Coventry, for example, the Mayor and Mayoress had already set up a fund for the alleviation of distress in the city and it was reported that more than £5,000 had been raised by 13th August. The Mayoress also launched a Shilling Fund to buy winter garments – or material that could be turned into garments – for needy women and children. However, by 21st August, Siegfried Bettmann was also acknowledging the receipt of more than £6,000, raised in Coventry as part of the Prince of Wales' Fund. In Rugby, a meeting of the Rugby UDC, on 11th August, was attended by Mr Nisbet, an inspector of the LGB, who explained the purpose of the Prince of Wales' Fund. It was intended, he said, as a national fund to ensure that richer districts should help the poorer ones. The Council took the decision to fall in line and Mr McKinnell was soon writing to the *Rugby Advertiser* explaining that money raised would go to a central fund and would not be used for local needs. He urged the people of Rugby to support the Fund. Coventry proved more resistant to the idea that money from the Prince of Wales' Fund should not be administered locally and there was a "sharp tussle" between Siegfried Bettmann and the London headquarters of the Fund. The Mayor was adamant that local funds should pass through local hands and administration should be carried out by those who knew the city's needs. The preference in London was to work through The Soldiers' and Sailors' Families Association. "Happily", as the *Coventry Herald* for 28th-29th August reported, "the officials at the London headquarters have now brought themselves into order." In Kenilworth, it was decided that money raised locally should be passed to the Prince of Wales' Fund and the town would then apply through the County Committee for grants that might be required.

Newspapers routinely carried lists of those donating to the Prince of Wales' Relief Fund and other worthy causes, with the amounts that each person had contributed being recorded. In Rugby, house to house collections were organised in support of the Prince of Wales' Fund. It was proposed to visit each house in the town and to encourage weekly donations of 1d – or more in the case of larger houses.

The initial impact of the war on local businesses varied quite considerably. The *Coventry Herald* for 14th-15th August carried a round-up of news from the local factories. Not surprisingly, a number were fully employed dealing with Government orders, such as Daimler, Herbert's and the Ordnance Works. Others were finding the situation more difficult: Coventry Chain was on short time but there had been no dismissals; Rudge-Whitworth had reduced the number of hours worked but still had a fair amount of work. The Singer Motor and Cycle Company was almost as busy as ever and the Triumph Company was operating near to normal. Messrs J. & J. Cash Ltd were working full time in most departments and benefiting from large numbers of orders for red, white and blue ribbons, and for Union Jacks. In Rugby, B.T.H. had brought workers back from holiday to deal with Admiralty orders for lamps and electrical plant used in dockyards etc. Other employers were opting for short time rather than discharging their workers. In Nuneaton, there was some initial concern but, by 28th August, the *Nuneaton Observer* was reporting that it did not look as though there would be any great distress locally; however, it added that employers of male labour seemed in agreement that, if any hands had to be discharged through lack of work, then it should be the young men capable of bearing arms who should go first, leaving the men of "more mature years with wives and families" to maintain production. One consequence of the outbreak of war was that a threatened strike among coal miners at Arley was called off, though the settlement involved the Arley Colliery Company accepting the demand of the Warwickshire Miners' Association that miners should belong to one association only. On 28th August, the *Leamington Spa Courier* was reporting that the war had not yet had a serious effect upon employment in the Leamington and Warwick area, although there had been a slight falling off in the building trade. The *Warwick Advertiser* (15th August) reported that many establishments were cutting down on the numbers of domestic servants, or even dispensing with their services altogether.

By the end of August, there was also a growing awareness that war would provide opportunities as well as difficulties. A 'magneto famine' immediately affected the British and French motor trades, which were dependent on imports from Germany, and a meeting was held in Coventry during the second week of August with a view to producing magnetos in Britain. By the end of the month, the *Coventry Herald* was drawing attention to the opportunities presenting themselves to Coventry's industry. "The continental motor and cycle industries have gone by the board and every effort should be made to capture them."[36] It was an indication of the way in which the area, like the country as a whole, was adjusting to the new situation.

Of course, the newspapers and the authorities were keen to offer assurances from the time that war broke out. The *Coventry Herald* (7th-8th August) reported that there was no panic at the news of war, events were "regarded even cheerfully". The following week, under the heading "Businesslike Coventry", the same newspaper commended the city's inhabitants for behaving "with exemplary calmness". There had been no fuss or bustle, and no "beating of the big drum" in connection with recruiting. "When at a later date the local events of the period are put on record the historian will have nothing but admiration for the way in which Coventry citizens met a situation in point of gravity without parallel in the lives of the oldest of them." By the third week of the war, the *Coventry Herald* was noting a marked change in the conditions of Coventry's streets. Although the evening crowds continued, they were smaller and less exuberant, in part because of the departure of so many young men, a theme to which the newspaper returned the following week: "With the departure of troops there are not so many outward signs of war in Midland towns, though we are made conscious of the existence of hostilities in sundry ways."[37] The *Nuneaton Observer* (14th August) felt that "Nuneaton and district has risen to the occasion", although concerns were subsequently expressed about the slow pace of recruiting in the town (see above).

An advert in the *Nuneaton Observer* for 21st August drew attention to a sale at Baker Bros, purveyors of 'high-class clothing'. Their products, it was claimed, were "Like The British Army, Always To The Front". In fact, the British people had little idea at all as to where the British Army was for most of August 1914, and only a scant idea of how the war was going in general. Both the Admiralty and the War Office censored the news. Henry Wilkins, in his Journal entry for 18th August, noted that: "The British Army has disappeared from public view". The *Stratford-upon-Avon Herald* (21st August) said that: "A thick blanket of silence has been spread over the entire theatre of war". Newspapers did the best they could by publishing the 'War Telegrams' but these can have offered little real information: "It is officially stated that the Germans in Alsace are retreating to the Rhine, and that the

French have captured 24 guns"; "The Belgians have retired to an entrenched position" etc.[38] The occasional article offered encouragement but not always accurate news: "8,000 Germans Killed. Brave Belgians Rout The Enemy At Liege" – or sometimes simply speculation: "Big Battle Imminent In The North Sea: Heavy Firing Heard At Grimsby".[39] The *Warwick Advertiser* carried a summary of 'This Week's Events' but, until the end of the month, the newspaper had little to report. Accompanying maps were conspicuous by their absence in the local press, which might explain the "Despicable Theft" of maps of northern Europe from the Atlas in the Reference Department of the Free Library in Nuneaton.[40] Given the lack of news, it was hardly surprising that rumours spread. Perhaps the most famous was the story about Russian troops landing in Britain, en route for the Western Front. Henry Wilkins recorded the rumour in his entries for the 29th and 30th August; one variation being that the Russians had, in fact been working in Scottish coal mines before being released for service. Wilkins himself gave scant credence to the story, though recording that: "all around the Midlands there are reports of a very large number of trains having passed from North to South during the weekend". On hearing that Russian troops had been seen at Leamington Station, Cordelia Leigh, along with friends and members of her family, travelled by motor and pony cart to Leamington on 29th August. No Russians were spotted – only some Yeomanry recruits going to Hereford – but they were assured by various people that the rumour was true and that, according to one account, "two Russian Officers had been seen in the streets".[41]

In Coventry and Warwickshire the outbreak of war had been accompanied by excitement, coupled with a degree of panic. The departure of the Army Reservists took place quickly, as well-laid plans were enacted. In their absence, the Territorials became the focus of patriotic feeling, somewhat ironic in view of the widespread condescension shown towards the 'Saturday Night Soldiers' before the war. Now they were the 'local Tommies', who "in their nation's need have forsaken employment, home comforts and domestic interests. ... People who have sneered at the Territorials must now see how valuable are these men."[42] Their departure from the area was witnessed by large crowds, even if the initial destinations of the soldiers were only places such as Swindon and Bury St Edmunds. The recruitment drive for the Kitchener's New Army produced a number of major meetings – that in Nuneaton estimated to be the largest in the history of the town – but enlistment was, at first, steady rather than dramatic and certainly did not compare with the scenes in Birmingham, where "the rush to the colours ... started on August 6th, and the assistance of the police had to be obtained in order to marshal the crowd outside the recruiting headquarters in James Watt Street".[43] However, the local situation changed dramatically in the week beginning Monday, 31st August, with a sudden increase in the numbers enlisting. In Coventry, for example, enlistment, which had been running at about 20 a day, suddenly jumped to 104 on 31st August, the start of a "tremendous boom"[44].

The initial panic, of which the most obvious manifestation was the stockpiling of food, does not appear to have lasted long. Throughout the region, councils met quickly to allay fears and consider measures to deal with the expected economic dislocation. In the event, these fears generally proved exaggerated, although some businesses did suffer from the loss of markets and the interruption to trading routes. Firms seem to have been quick to consider how home produced alternatives might be found for goods previously imported from Germany. Despite concerns, the harvest was successfully gathered in, sometimes with the help of volunteers. Nonetheless, distress committees were soon formed (or reconvened) and people contributed freely to funds, especially to that set up at the behest of the Prince of Wales.

What was readily apparent was the desire on the part of many people in the area to make some sort of contribution to the war effort. "Nearly everyone with any time to spare now seems anxious to help the country", said the *Warwick Advertiser* (15th August). For women, this took the form of traditional tasks, such as knitting and rolling bandages or training as nurses. It was a far cry from the major role that women would play in the war effort that saw thousands of women employed by 1918 in local industries. Patriotic men vied with Boy Scouts to protect vulnerable localities and to assist the authorities. Given the quickly stated opposition of the War Office to local defence forces, it tended to be the Scouts who found themselves the busier, the start of a long and honourable effort on the part of the Scouting movement during the war. Like the Red Cross Society, the Scouts benefited from the fact that their organisation already existed. Moreover, it was one which was "simple and fluid and which would allow it to fill gaps in public service. Many such gaps appeared as the nation moved quickly from peace to war."[45] It also helped that the war began at the start of the school holidays and that many Scouts had assembled at their annual camp. (Local defence forces did re-emerge later in the year, as a more co-ordinated scheme of Volunteer Training Corps, affiliated to the Central Volunteer Training Association. For example, one was formed at Rugby in December 1914. In addition, many men joined the rifle clubs that burgeoned in the autumn of 1914, such as the one formed at Kenilworth in September.)

The rising price of food stuffs was an early indication of the difficulties that lay ahead. Restrictions on people's freedom tended to be limited at this early stage of the war, unless, of course, the person was deemed an 'alien'. On 8th August, Parliament passed the Defence of the Realm Act, which conferred on the Government widespread powers, including trial by courts martial for civilians (amended in March 1915). A second act was passed on 28th August. Although the acronym DORA would become instantly recognisable at a later stage, it appears absent from the coverage of the war by local newspapers during August 1914.

Everywhere, the war was the dominant subject of conversation, already exercising "its huge gravitational pull".[46] In Brinklow, "the only subject of conversation over the last week has been 'The War'"; in Long Itchington "War news is the one engrossing topic. It is eagerly discussed by men, women and even schoolchildren."[47] In Warwick "everyone has been giving up all other topics of conversation for the one great topic of the day – the war, what it means, and what it may mean."[48] Some clearly welcomed the unifying effect that the war was having. Industrial unrest and the threat of civil war in Ireland seemed to have disappeared. "There exists a true conception of Christian brotherhood throughout the land", said the Rev. J. Cairns to his parishioners at St Nicholas' Church in Kenilworth.[49] Dissenting voices, of course, struggled to be heard; rather, it was those who had no doubts as to the justice of the cause whose views received an airing. Thus the Rev. P.M. Herbert, preaching at the Parish Church in Rugby, on 2nd August: "better a thousand time a disastrous war than a dishonourable peace".[50]

There was no "phoney war" in 1914: the major protagonists soon clashed. The Battle of the Frontiers left France with more than a quarter of a million casualties by the end of August. In the east, the Battle of Tannenburg between the German and Russian armies began on August 23rd. However, it was not until the end of the month that news came through of the involvement of the British Expeditionary Force at Mons on 23rd August: "British Troops in First Big Battle".[51] Detail, however, was short, although the *Leamington Spa Courier* reported that there had been 2,000 British casualties, slightly more than was the case. There had already been losses at sea, notably the sinking of HMS *Amphion* on 6th August. (Those lost included a grandson of Mr Davis Hunt, a Southam magistrate.) Nonetheless, despite the scant reporting of events, it must have seemed in these early weeks that the war was being fought by Britain's allies, as essentially it was. By comparison with the months that lay ahead, it is the lengthening lists of local casualties that are conspicuous by their absence. Instead, attention tended to focus on the fate of those civilians who had found themselves trapped abroad when the war broke out. Most returned safely – including Henry Wilkins' daughter – and several passed on their experiences to the local newspapers, their stories appearing under headings such as 'Exciting Journey'. Some, such as Mr Ivor Hart, a Leamington science master, had witnessed the fighting in Belgium. However, not all were able to return home: for example, Mr George Bainton, a well-known composer and musician, who had gone to Bayreuth to attend the Wagner festival, was to spend the war in a civilian prisoner of war camp in Germany. Otherwise, it was those local servicemen who had suffered accidents whose stories were being reported, such as William Smith, from Kenilworth, who was accidentally shot by a sentry whilst garrisoned at Gibraltar. Inevitably, the full implications of Britain's involvement war were not apparent in these early weeks.

Instead, August 1914 provides an insight into local attitudes towards the war, before the casualties began. The phrase 'business as usual' was being used in London by the end of the second week of the war and the sentiment appeared locally at about the same time, even if it had not yet become a catchphrase. Thus the *Stratford-upon-Avon Herald*, 14th August, supported the appeal made by the town's leaders "to keep cool, to go about one's business as usual". Such advice, however, reflects a concern to minimise the impact of the war rather than a record of what was actually happening. The outbreak of war was accompanied by a remarkable burst of activity, as people sought ways to support the national cause; it also had a disruptive effect and the large amounts of money quickly donated to relief funds suggest an expectation that distress would be widespread and quite possibly long-lasting. Any hopes that the war might be short were soon challenged by Kitchener's campaign to raise a new army and by the widespread support for that campaign. Suggestions the war would be 'over by Christmas' were conspicuous by their absence. However, like the ever lengthening casualty lists, the extensive integration of the British economy and society into the war effort lay in the future. The perceived role of local people in these early weeks was to rally behind the armed forces and those in authority. The contemporary historian, R.H. Gretton, said of Britain in the early months of the Great War, that it "was not a nation at war but a nation supporting and encouraging part of itself at war".[52] It is an observation that still seems valid.

CB

---

1 Arthur Marwick: "The Deluge: British Society and the First World War"; Macmillan Press, 1965

2 Henry Charles Wilkins: "Journal of the Great European War" Coventry History Centre JN940.3

3 Quoted in Gordon H. Maycock: "The Triumph of Siegfried Bettmann"; Coventry Branch of the Historical Association, 2000

4 Cordelia Leigh: "Diary of the War", Shakespeare Centre and Library DR671/510

5 Henry Wilkins: op. cit.

6 *Rugby Advertiser*, 8th August, 1914

7 *Coventry Herald*, 7th-8th August, 1914

8 *Coventry Herald*, 7th-8th August, 1914

9 Cordelia Leigh: op. cit.

10 *Coventry Herald*, 7th-8th August, 1914

11 *Coventry Herald*, 7th-8th August, 1914

12 Charles Messenger: "Call-To-Arms", Weidenfeld & Nicolson, 2005

13 *Coventry Herald*, 7th-8th, 1914

14 In effect, the local companies were half-companies, numbering eight per battalion, rather than the four that would subsequently be the norm.

15 *The Observer*, 7th August, 1914

the market square. After the German soldiers moved on, people fled, as the soldiers had promised that they would return. They trudged from village to village before many eventually reached Antwerp. From there, they had taken a boat to Tilbury.

As the number of refugees coming to Rugby increased, so other properties were offered as homes. Mrs Little made The Lodge at Clifton upon Dunsmore available for a party that was expected by the end of October. Mr Henry Boughton-Leigh offered Newton House, near Rugby. Subsequently, Mr Kittermaster offered, unfurnished, 17 Hillmorton Road and, initially, 25 refugees moved in; this number had increased to 40 by March 1915. Another property to be offered was The Beeches, in Clifton, owned by Mr Buzzard.

In January 1915, it was stated in the *Rugby Advertiser* that a further 25 refugees had arrived at Clifton, following a visit to Alexandra Palace in London by Mr Mulliner and Mr F. Van Der Arend, Secretary of the Newton House War Relief Fund.[4] The Palace was used to hold those refugees who still needed homes, of whom there were several thousand in early 1915. Refugees crowded around the two men, imploring to be taken. Many were agricultural labourers, who would no doubt be warmly welcomed as replacements for British men who had gone into the Army. The basis upon which the 25 newcomers were selected is unclear, but they included three men who were, respectively, a wheelwright, a cabinet maker and a cigar maker. The men were accompanied by their wives and children.

4. Refugees Arrive at Coventry

Refugees began to arrive in Coventry in October 1914. Many took up rooms vacated by local men who had enlisted, but Belgian families were often large and the problem of where to house these families was not so easy to solve. Parents obviously wished to stay with their children but facilities for housing such families were few and far between. One solution was the offer to use Whitley Abbey made by Colonel Oswald Henry Turville-Petre. The Lord Mayor, Mr Siegfried Bettman, JP, negotiated the loan of the property as a refuge for those arriving in the country. The Abbey was located in the leafy outskirts of Coventry. Once the home of the Hood family, then the Wheelers and finally the Petre family, it had not been used since the death of Lady Gwendoline Petre in 1910. Younger members of the family, having adopted the name of Turville-Petre, had moved to Bosworth Hall, near Market Bosworth, but still owned the Abbey. The grounds served as a playground for the local Whitley children and the house lay empty and lacking its former glory.

As elsewhere, Coventry people were most anxious to help those less fortunate than themselves and responded wholeheartedly to requests for furniture, clothes, food and other necessities to make the empty Abbey at Whitley suitable for habitation once again. Local churches requested their congregations to donate what they could, both in terms of goods and money. A special committee was set up, chaired by the Rev. Canon Baillie, to prepare the Abbey and there was also a considerable input from the local landed gentry, including members of the Hood family and Colonel Wyley, the High Sheriff, as well as local businessmen and Councillors. A sub-committee of ladies was formed to sort items of furniture, bedding and clothes, and to ensure that the Abbey was ready for the arrival of the refugees in early October. The idea was to fit out the building as far as possible in the style to which the refugees were accustomed and to create a 'home from home'. The fact that the Abbey had a Catholic Chapel on site proved an additional bonus in this respect, as the party were of the Catholic faith and led by a priest, Father Truyens, and three Sisters from a teaching order.

A week's hard work on the part of an energetic group of ladies transformed the accommodation at Whitley Abbey, which was ready to receive the first party of 22 refugees, who arrived on the afternoon of 7th October. The authorities did their best to keep the arrival of the Belgians a secret but many local people anticipated what was happening and about 300 gathered at Coventry Station. The initial party was made up of three families of nine, seven and six members, who came from the Malines and Termonde districts of Belgian. None of them could speak English and they had very few possessions with them, just a few "pathetic packages", according to the *Coventry Herald*.[5] Nonetheless, the refugees seemed healthy and cheerful and were quickly conveyed to their new home, with which they were suitably delighted.

The first refugees at Coventry were described by the local newspaper as "a nice class of work people"[6], and the expectation was that more large families would be accommodated at the Abbey. The refugees had not come directly from London but had spent a night in Birmingham before travelling to Coventry. By the time of their arrival, more than 70 beds had been made available at the Abbey, with another 40 or so in reserve. The buildings had been divided into two separate wings, one for the men and the other for the women and children. The men were provided with a recreation room, in which it was intended to place a billiards table, and the children were given a play room, as well as enjoying access to a large area of grass outside the buildings. Three Sisters from the Ursuline Convent at Puers, near Antwerp, accompanied the party of 22, having also escaped from the advancing German troops. The Sisters belonged to a teaching order and the plan was to provide a school for an anticipated 60-70 children.

The numbers at the Abbey soon increased, though arrangements did not always go according to plan. There was a breakdown in communications with the authorities in London, with the result that two parties arrived at short notice on 11th October; both proved unsuitable to the Coventry authorities. The first, a group of 27, consisted of youngish married couples of professional and business people, for whom there was no adequate provision at the Abbey, the thinking of the Coventry committee being that the Abbey should cater for large families of "the peasant and working class". The second party, of 17, were, in fact, sent to Coventry by mistake, their intended destination being Cardiff. Most of the newcomers accepted the situation cheerfully enough and a number would subsequently find more suitable accommodation with Coventry families. However, one couple "proved utterly unaccommodating". They would not eat the food, were rude to the nuns and the priest and said that they expected to be taken to a rich home and made comfortable; in fact, "they behaved like silly, spoilt children".[7] They were soon sent back to London, their behaviour so out of keeping with that of the other refugees that it was later reported that they had been placed under police supervision in London, on suspicion that they were, in fact, Germans![8]

The refugees at Whitley Abbey came mainly from Antwerp, Mechlin and Louvain; by the end of October, as many as 120 had been admitted to the Abbey. The day to day running of the operation, together with the monitoring of orders and finance, were in the hands of a Mr Charles Frederick Mast, who had been appointed Honorary Superintendent by the Committee. His wife, Evelyn, is thought to have been instrumental in co-ordinating the activities of the Ladies Committee.

5. Refugees Arrive at Kenilworth

In October 1914, the County Committee appealed to local clergy to help the Belgian Refugees. The Rev. Cairns, vicar of St Nicholas parish church in Kenilworth, and his wife were already involved in helping the refugees and had opened up a depot in the town to receive gifts of clothing, which would be forwarded to the Central Organisation. Rev. Cairns now thought it might be practicable to take an empty house in Kenilworth, furnish it and provide for a considerable number of refugees and so he called a meeting in the Parochial Hall to discuss the situation.[9] At the packed meeting, the vicar proposed that Bridge House, a large dwelling on the corner of Coventry Road, be taken for about 20 middle-class Belgian refugees. He already had been in touch with the County Distress

Committee on the subject and had informed them that little could be done in Kenilworth in the way of providing for the peasant class, as all cottages were occupied, but that there was a large empty house which could be utilised for entertaining a higher social class. However, he had been told by the Committee that, at present, there were no refugees of that class not provided for.

The ownership of Bridge House was in a state of transition but Mr Lawrence, the purchaser, had generously offered the house at a rent representing 4% of his outlay. Funds would be needed to fit out the house but, taking into account doubtless gifts of vegetables and other articles, Rev. Cairns estimated that 20 refugees could be maintained for six months for a sum not exceeding £200. He had already received most encouraging letters on the subject and offers of subscriptions to a very considerable amount. He was anxious to enlist the sympathy and practical assistance of all classes in this scheme and proposed to invite weekly subscriptions down to 1s per week, so that all could feel they were taking a hand in helping the unfortunate refugees. The meeting supported the proposed initiative and a resolution was passed and power given to a Committee for augmenting the proposals should funds and opportunities offer. A Finance Committee was appointed and also a Management Committee, with the vicar presiding over these. All those on the Finance Committee were men; those on the Management Committee were all ladies, apart from the vicar. Nearly £200 was subscribed that night.

The period following the meeting was very busy. Unperturbed by the County Committee's statement that there were no refugees of a higher social class awaiting accommodation, the day after the meeting Rev. and Mrs Cairns visited the headquarters for the Belgian refugees at Aldwich, London. They interviewed and made arrangements for 21 refugees to be sent to Kenilworth on Saturday of the following week. These would be mostly of the professional classes, and a priest, Canon Van den Broeck, was also to be included in the party. The whole of the group were acquaintances and were delighted to have the opportunity of living together. Prior to their arrival, a Finance and Management Committee had been formed in the town. At Bridge House, painters and tradesmen were soon at work, rooms were cleaned and van loads of furniture arrived as townspeople provided chairs, carpets, curtains, pictures and other articles needed to make the accommodation habitable. Several ladies undertook to furnish one room in its entirety whilst Mrs Kay, who was leaving Kenilworth for a while, was good enough to lend most of her furniture.[10]

On 24th October, 18 of the 21 expected refugees arrived at Kenilworth Station at midday, whence they were conveyed by motor cars and carriages to Bridge House. The party was made up of four families and "two or three unattached individuals". Large crowds had met the refugees on their arrival in Kenilworth, both at the Station and at Bridge House. The leaders of the Belgian party raised their hats and smiled a greeting, but quiet and unobtrusive sympathy was the dominant note in the behaviour of the Kenilworth people. Inside Bridge House, the refugees were welcomed by the Management Committee and also by the Rev. Canon Caswell and Dr Loxton. Rev. Cairns spoke in French and extended a most hearty welcome on behalf of the Kenilworth inhabitants. There were to be no rules of the house, which was open to the refugees to use as a home from home. He regretted his Church was not in communion with their Church and introduced Canon Caswell of the Roman Catholic Church. He asked them to choose one of their number to confer with the Committee on any point arising and also a lady to conduct household affairs with Mrs Chandler.

Canon Van den Broeck, of Malines Cathedral, replied (in French). He described the terrible sufferings they had undergone, their losses, their bereavements, their helplessness and almost hopelessness. He described how he was sitting in his study when the first bombardment of Malines commenced and three shells fell in rapid succession on his house. He gathered a few things and fled to Bruges. The first bombardment of Malines having ceased, he returned, and found his home in ruins, out of which he saved a few trifles; he then returned to Bruges. On the fall of Antwerp, the people in Bruges fled to Ostend and, on the day of the arrival of the Germans there, his party managed to board a crowded boat. They arrived in Dover Harbour where they were kept with insufficient food and under indescribable conditions for two days before being permitted to leave, as it was feared that German spies were on board. The whole party had scarcely a penny among them and had only the few summer clothes in which they stood. Canon Van den Broeck subsequently wrote a letter to the local newspaper, which was printed both in French and English thanking the Committee and people of Kenilworth in the name of his Belgian fellow countrymen for their welcome. He explained some of the suffering they had recently undergone and now hoped that their presence in the midst of their new fellow-citizens would be both a source of happiness and new prosperity, and forge more strongly the bonds of brotherhood that already united the English and Belgian nations.[11]

Over £400 had been collected in the few days since the public meeting and many people who were unable to give large subscriptions were contributing in kind, with provisions such as vegetables, fruit and household requisites. In fact, the response of the townsfolk had been so good there was a suggestion from the Finance Committee of opening another home a little later on, probably at the other end of Kenilworth. Picking up on this suggestion, an editorial comment in the *Kenilworth Advertiser* suggested that now this party of refugees were settled perhaps an effort would be made to assist a party of Belgians of the poorer classes, even though there were no suitable houses vacant for them and it did not seem possible to board them singly because of the difficulty of understanding their wants, as the peasant classes spoke only Flemish. However, no other house was ever set up.[12]

6. The Public Response to the Refugees

In Rugby, concern for the newcomers was mixed with curiosity. Many local people made their way to Clifton to see the refugees and sympathise with them. Some brought gifts. However, the committee looking after the refugees decided that the strain of so many visitors was not good for the Belgians, with the result that, in future, people had to obtain clearance from the committee before making a visit. In October, a plea was made for help with goods and for money. Transport was offered for furniture that was heavy. Further appeals for the loan of furniture were made in December and in January 1915. Items requested ranged from beds, of which 40 were required, to candle stands, cooking utensils, knives, forks and spoons. It was suggested that employees of local firms might equip a complete room and have it named after their company. Staff at the *Rugby Advertiser* offered to make donations to enable useful items to be purchased.[13]

For the first few months after their arrival, there was considerable interest shown in the activities of the refugees. Take, for example, the coverage in the *Rugby Advertiser* of the wedding, in November 1914, of Victor Buelens and Emilie Alice Dekeyser. The couple originally came from Louvain and their marriage had been planned before the war. They had already acquired a house but this had been lost, along with wedding presents and nearly all their clothes. However, their wedding now proceeded at St Marie's Church in Rugby. Alice was a costumier, who had run a flourishing business in Belgium, with her two sisters; naturally, she made her own wedding dress. Victor, who was originally a printer by trade, had already found employment at the British Thomson-Houston (B.T.H.) works. The wedding was well-attended, with, presumably, many local citizens present. The paper doubted whether "the beautiful church of St Marie's had ever held such a large congregation for a nuptial ceremony". The service was presided over by a Belgian priest, Father Lerude.[14]

In Coventry, Whitley Abbey remained in use for the duration of the war. When the war ended and most of the refugees returned home, the Abbey again fell empty, although cottages and farms belonging to the estate were still occupied. By 1924 steps were taken to sell the property but it remained unoccupied and gradually deteriorated. In the 1950s, Coventry Council took over the Abbey as the site for a new comprehensive school; Whitley Abbey School opened in 1955. All traces of the old Abbey and its chapel, which were first recorded on a map of 1360, have now disappeared. However, memories of its former peace and tranquillity will no doubt have lived on among the Belgian refugees who had stayed there during the First World War. In 1920, the King of Belgium awarded Charles and Evelyn Mast medals for their services to the refugees; the medals are now held by the Mast's granddaughter, Mrs Peggy Bloom, of Coventry.

---

[1] *Coventry Herald*, 11th-12th September, 1914
[2] *Rugby Advertiser*, 3rd October, 1914
[3] *Rugby Advertiser*, 3rd October, 1914
[4] *Rugby Advertiser*, 23rd January, 1915
[5] *Coventry Herald* 9th-10th October, 1914
[6] *Coventry Herald* 9th-10th October, 1914
[7] *Coventry Herald*, 16th-17th October, 1914
[8] *Coventry Herald*, 23rd-24th October, 1914
[9] *The Kenilworth Advertiser*, 17th October, 1914
[10] *The Kenilworth Advertiser*, 24th October, 1914
[11] *The Kenilworth Advertiser*, 31st October, 1914
[12] *The Kenilworth Advertiser*, 31st October, 1914
[13] *Rugby Advertiser*, 2nd January, 1915
[14] *Rugby Advertiser*, 28th November, 1914
[15] *Coventry Herald* 9th-10th October, 1914
[16] *Coventry Herald*, 23rd-24th October, 1914
[17] *The Kenilworth Advertiser*, 31st October, 1914
[18] *The Kenilworth Advertiser*, 21st November, 1914
[19] *The Kenilworth Advertiser*, 2nd January, 1915
[20] *Rugby Advertiser*, 20th February, 1915
[21] *Rugby Advertiser*, 12th August 1916
[22] *Rugby Advertiser*, 16th January 1915
[23] *Rugby Advertiser*, 20th February, 1915
[24] Admissions register, Wheatley Street School, Coventry History Centre CCE/COL3/3/5
[25] *Coventry Herald*, 23rd-24th October, 1914
[26] *The Kenilworth Advertiser*, 7th November 1914
[27] *Rugby Advertiser*, 7th February, 1915
[28] *Rugby Advertiser*, 10th July 1915
[29] Henry Charles Wilkins: "Journal of the Great European War", Coventry History Centre JN940.3
[30] *The Kenilworth Advertiser*, 1st April, 1916
[31] The Kenilworth Advertiser, 19th December, 1914
[32] Arthur Marwick: "The Deluge"; Macmillan Press, 1965
[33] *Rugby Advertiser*, 30th December, 1916
[34] *The Kenilworth Advertiser*, 21st July, 1916
[35] *The Kenilworth Advertiser*, 12th August, 1916
[36] *The Kenilworth Advertiser*, 16th November, 1918

Chapter 3

Recruitment

The raising of the 216th Fortress Company in Nuneaton in 1915

James Sambrook

James Sambrook

☙

'The Lord he created the Engineer,
Her Majesty's Royal Engineer,
With the rank and pay of a Sapper.'

Nuneaton's Company of Royal Engineers was made not by Kipling's Lord but by Lord Kitchener, Secretary of State for War, and Alderman W.T. Bates, Mayor of Nuneaton. Nuneaton men had responded to Kitchener's call for volunteers at the beginning of the war, so that before the end of October 1914 the number of the town's recruits to Kitchener's 'New Army' was equivalent to two battalions (including more than a thousand men who enlisted in the first week of September), but no specific 'Pals' Battalion' of infantry, similar to those raised by civic pride and patriotism in other English towns, was recruited in Nuneaton. By 1915, static trench warfare on the Western Front revealed a shortage of support units, especially artillery and engineers, so, in late January and early February, the War Office made a renewed appeal to the 'pals' battalion' sentiment by sending to local authorities up and down the country a 'shopping list' of the kinds of units now required for the Army. Nuneaton Borough Council having chosen the engineers, the Mayor was authorized (30 March 1915) to raise a company to be known as the 216th Fortress Company, Royal Engineers (Nuneaton).* The Borough Council was required to provide uniforms (made by local clothing firms) and to feed, pay, and lodge the members of this company, but these costs would be eventually refunded by the War Office. The Mayor was given authority to nominate a Commanding Officer; his choice fell on Mr F.C.

* The traditional function of Royal Engineer `Fortress' companies was to build and maintain fixed defences. However, the Nuneaton company's title was changed from 216th Fortress Company to 216th Army Troops Company very soon after they left Nuneaton in August 1915. The change, which was made with few exceptions to Fortress Companies throughout the Corps, reflected the multiple new functions of a body that would operate in the field, rather than in garrison fortresses.

Cook, the Borough Surveyor, a willing volunteer who was given leave of absence by the Council for as long as the Army needed him. The War Office granted him a temporary commission as a captain on 14 April.[1]

Similar arrangements were being made all over Great Britain in response to the War Office shopping list. The 216th was one of forty-eight Royal Engineer companies raised locally during 1915 by town councils, among which were Nuneaton's neighbours Rugby and Coventry. These companies were mostly officered by passably healthy civilian engineers who had practical experience in supervising engineering work of some kind or another. Knowledge of soldiering was to be acquired later, though Captain Cook was not devoid of military experience, for he had been a sergeant in the Territorials, also Commandant of the Nuneaton Church Lads' Brigade before 1900, and, more recently, Commandant of the Nuneaton Citizens' Training Corps.[2] He was forty years old in 1915: well above the average age for an Army captain.

At the time the Nuneaton Company was formed, the war was more than seven months old. The country had taken note of Lord Kitchener's demand for volunteers on the famous poster, with fierce eyes and a peremptory gloved finger pointing directly at the poor guilty shirker, proclaiming that the army 'wants YOU', and Nuneaton's patriotic newspapers had added their shrill reinforcement. The *Nuneaton Observer*, for instance, announced the outbreak of war with the headline: 'St. George and the Dragon. Europe's United Fight against the Mad Dictator. Britain Unsheathes the Sword in a Just Cause. King and Country's Call to Nuneaton's Young Men.' Every local newspaper published a weekly 'Roll of Honour' listing names of the latest recruits. Recruiting advertisements assured Nuneaton's young men that, if they enlisted, they would command their country's gratitude after the War and be looked up to and respected because they answered their country's call. No man could win a Victoria Cross by staying away from the recruiting office. 'The Regiments at the Front are covering themselves with Glory.' 'Enter your name today on the Nation's Roll of Honour and do your part. God save the King.'[3]

The kind of glory that many men were covered in was revealed by the accompanying reports of Nuneaton men (regulars, reservists, Territorials, mostly in the Royal Warwickshire Regiment) killed and missing on active service in places whose names would become miserably familiar over the next four years. The war had not ended by Christmas 1914, as many had predicted; but the British High Command, with the notable exception of the Secretary of State for War, Earl Kitchener himself, still imagined that it would be a short contest, characterized by movement and a knock-out blow. On 22 January 1915 Sir Douglas Haig, commanding the British First Army in France, told *The Times* military correspondent that as soon as his artillery were supplied with ample ammunition 'we could walk through the German lines at several places'.[4] The generals were confident that a really strong frontal assault would bring swift victory in 1915, but in retrospect it is clear that on the Western Front, where facing lines of strongly defended trenches ran from Switzerland to the North Sea, the war had reached stalemate. The High Command were slow to realize that the struggle on the Western Front was primarily a monstrous siege operation: an engineers' war.

Nuneaton's recruiting office was in the Law Courts/Police Station building on the corner of Coton Road and Chapel Street. The recruiting officer was Major George MacMullen, ex-Indian Army, 59 years old, and lodging at the Windsor Temperance Hotel; his son was serving with the Army in France.[5] There were recruiting offices also in Atherstone and Bedworth. Most men enlisted in the Royal Warwickshire Regiment, but many other units also found recruits in Nuneaton, despite the local papers' incessant complaints about 'shirkers' who would not come forward to answer the appeal of King and Country. For instance, though Arthur Daulman, Wilf Cox, and Ernie Addison came out of the recruiting office as Royal Engineers of the 216th Company, they had entered it with the intention of joining the Scottish Rifles, influenced, said Daulman, by 'the Scots uniform and jaunty headgear'.[6]

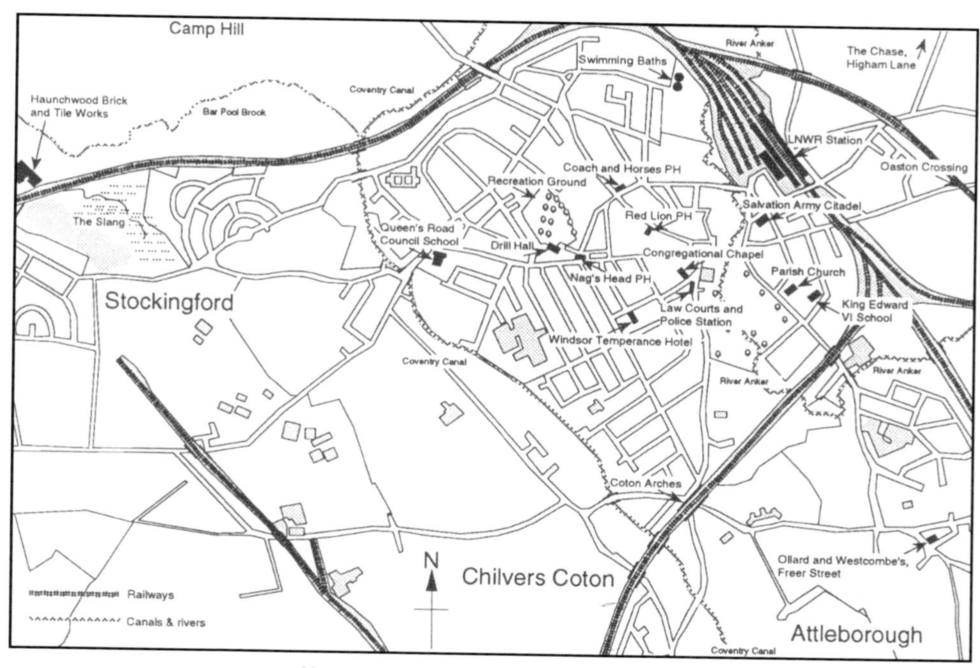

Nuneaton at the time of the Great War.

Men too old or medically unfit for enlistment in the regular armed forces of the Crown could enrol in the Nuneaton Citizens' Training Corps and so join the million or so men in similar units up and down the country receiving instruction in musketry and drill. For youngsters, aged between 16 and 19, there was a Nuneaton Junior Citizens' Training Corps, launched in the hall of the King Edward VI Grammar School on 23 November 1914, on the motion of Charles Streather, a recent old boy, now a pupil-teacher at Queen's Road Council School. He said 'there were many youths about who, although willing and eager to join the army, were not yet old enough. In case of sudden attack these would at present be useless, but with organization and drilling they would soon make valuable units of defence. Again would it not be much better, not only for the army but for the recruits themselves, if by the time they were old enough to enlist, they had already become fairly proficient in their work.' Streather already had a list of nearly a hundred boys and had been promised the use of two halls and a miniature rifle range.[7] As we shall see, the age-rule for enlistment into the real army proved, in practice, to be more elastic than was assumed in the age-range of the Junior Citizens' Training Corps.

The real soldiers most plain to view in Nuneaton during the early months of the war were three regular infantry battalions belonging to the 86th Brigade (29th Division), i.e. the 2nd Royal Fusiliers, the 1st Royal Dublin Fusiliers, and the 1st Lancashire Fusiliers. They had been brought home from India to be acclimatized, presumably for France, but their eventual destination proved to be Gallipoli; they were billeted in Nuneaton from January to March 1915. Arthur Daulman recalls: 'The Dubliners were at daggers drawn, bayonets drawn would be more appropriate, with one of the other battalions and they were indeed drawn in the Red Lion pub. The fracas was only put under control with difficulty.' They were not the only ones out of control, for he also recalls that 'Alderman Melly got into trouble at this time when he drove his gig through the ranks of marching men. The air was blue and he was in danger of being tipped up. He was subsequently fined £25.'

April saw the publication of an advertisement addressed 'To the Men of Nuneaton, Atherstone, and Bedworth', signed by the Mayor and Captain Cook, announcing that 'The War Office have authorized the raising of a Local (Fortress) Company of Royal Engineers for the New (Fifth) Army. 105 Non-Commissioned Officers and men are required immediately for the following trades: Shoeing and Carriage, Smiths, Drivers, Blacksmiths, Bricklayers, Carpenters, Clerks, Draughtsmen, Electricians, Engine Drivers, Fitters and Turners, Surveyors, Masons, Harness Makers, Platelayers, Plumbers, Wheelwrights.' The Mayor appealed confidently to the men of Nuneaton and district to join the Company 'and so effectively serve their King and Country in this Hour of Britain's Greatest Need.' The *Nuneaton Chronicle* backed this appeal with `psychological' speculations in an editorial on 16 April: 'Nuneaton, Bedworth and the surrounding districts have responded nobly to the Country's Call, but there are still men amongst us who have delayed to answer for reasons which can only be described as psychological. That is to say their hearts have insistently urged them to face their responsibilities as members of the glorious Empire to which they belong, but their minds have shrunk from becoming merely a numbered unit in the vast Kitchener's Army. These men have been ready and willing to defend the honour of England, but they wanted to feel they were doing something for their own friends and relatives here in Nuneaton. The opportunity now presents itself.'

The first two recruits were Sapper Joe Webster, a bricklayer, and Driver Bill Orrill; the next two were Wilf Cox and Ernie Addison, who both worked in signal-boxes at Nuneaton L.N.W.R. station; the fifth, as shown by his regimental number 92685 was Arthur Daulman, apprentice weaver at Ollard and Westcombe's factory in Freer Street, Attleborough. Daulman was a few weeks short of his seventeenth birthday, Cox was seventeen, and Addison eighteen, so they were all under the statutory minimum age of nineteen. Arthur Daulman recalled: 'First came the medical examination by Dr Nason, our family doctor, who did not spend much time on me. Then we were sworn in by the recruiting sergeant. He it was who probably had my shilling [the one the writer imagined would be given to each recruit]. At this time Capt. Cook entered and said: "Which is Daulman out of you three?" "Me sir." "How old are you?" "19." "Oh, all right." But I later found out that he had learnt that I was 16, because Mr Wells [the manager at Ollard and Westcombe's] phoned down and told him. Gert Saunders in the warehouse overheard the conversation and told me. When I got back home I told my mother and father. I can't print what my father said. He had been in the old Volunteers for many years and had attended thirteen camps in Stoneleigh. He never stopped me, although he could have done.' (The 'old Volunteers' were government-funded, locally organized, units in which civilians were given military training; they were absorbed into the new Territorial Army when this was formed in 1908.)

Another nineteen men joined the 216th Company, R.E. in the week to 23 April: Frank Adams, Billy Barratt, Len Brooks, Fred Duckerin, Bill Higham, Charles Lathbury, Len Marriott, Fred Mobbs, Joe Moreton, Tom Norman, James Parton, Herbert Ross, Ernest Shade, Albert Taylor, Arthur Taylor, Harry Trevis, Sol Walker, John Wheway, and Alf Wiggins. (Sapper Norman was destined to have the unenviable distinction of being the only member of the 216th Company to be captured by the enemy.) The *Nuneaton Observer* praised these and the thirty other men who joined other army formations that week.[8] It made much of one in particular, proclaiming in its usual style: 'Nuneaton's manhood who interest themselves in football have a great example to follow this week. "Billy" Barratt, the famous left back of Nuneaton Town, has enlisted in the local Fortress Company of Engineers. After he has helped Nuneaton to win the shield he is going to help the British Empire win the greatest of all wars. The best tribute to "Billy" Barratt's popularity will consist in him being followed to the recruiting station by 100 men. ... There is a glory and honour in being able to serve the nation in this the greatest crisis in history.' Nuneaton Town Football Club did, indeed, win the Birmingham Combination Shield that season. Their last match (a 5-2 victory) was at home on 1 May: Barratt scored two penalties and delivered a recruiting speech to the enthusiastic crowd at the end of the game: he said that Captain Cook had asked him to call for recruits to the Nuneaton Fortress Company and that the men especially wanted were blacksmiths, carpenters, plumbers, bricklayers, and masons.[9]

On 22 April the second battle of Ypres began with a German poison-gas attack. 25 April saw the first landings at Gallipoli, when, in the space of two days the 1st Royal Dublin Fusiliers lost all but four of their officers and over 550 men, and the other two battalions recently billeted in Nuneaton lost half their officers and over a third of their rank and file. Meanwhile, the Nuneaton Royal Engineers Company began drilling every morning and afternoon in the Drill Hall on the Recreation Ground; their instructor was Acting Sergeant Major Mitchinson, a regular reservist who had been recalled to the colours at the outbreak of war. He had joined the army in 1899, entering the Royal Field Artillery; he was promoted to sergeant in 1902 and transferred to the 1st Life Guards. He was placed on the Reserve in 1909 and joined the Birmingham City Police Force. On his recall he was posted to the Warwick depot as a drill instructor, so when he joined the 216 R.E. in April 1915 he was wearing the Royal Warwickshire's cap badge. He had the unusual distinction among British soldiers of having seen the Kaiser, because, during his service in the Life Guards, he had ridden in an escort for the German Emperor as well as for several other crowned heads.[10] Arthur Daulman called him a strict disciplinarian. Another recruit, Arthur Sambrook, said 'He fancied himself'.[11] It was likely to be an uneasy conjunction between this product of Edwardian military pageantry, the civilian workers and craftsmen turned soldiers now under his command, and, in France, the realities of a kind of warfare neither of the parties had ever dreamed of.

Before the middle of May another 35 local men had joined the 216th R.E. They were Cyril Anderton, Frank Arnold, Harry Ashley, John Barker, George Baxter, William Benson, John Collins, George Copson, Frank Cox, Alfred Evans, Ernie Fenn and his brother Sym, Frederick Follet, Charlie Harris, David Harrison, George ('Dick') Harvey, Frank Hextall, Sam Hollis, Allen Hughes, Harry Ludford, George ('Cubby') Marston, C.T. Montgomery, Fred Moore, Percy Phillips, Edwin and George Reader, Herbert Rees, Arthur Sambrook, Walter Shelmerdine, Fred Sherriff, Ernest Stone, Charlie Streather, Bill Toogood, Dick Townsend, and Alfred Wade. (Copson, Harvey, and Marston would all be killed in France within nine days of landing in that country.) Streather had been the prime mover in the foundation of the Nuneaton Junior Citizens' Training Corps six months earlier; he was now old enough officially to join the army. The *Nuneaton Chronicle* observed happily: 'The total strength of the Company is now 61. It is satisfactory to notice that carpenters have commenced to come forward, and that six are already enrolled. Men of this trade are still required to complete the establishment, as are blacksmiths and masons. There are also vacancies for a harness maker, plasterer, slater and wheelwright. Men are being served out with uniform and equipment immediately they join, and there is every reason to believe that (with the possible exception of masons) the Company will be brought up to full strength without the necessity of an appeal outside the Nuneaton Recruiting Area.' The uniform was regulation khaki, including a soft cap with flat crown: steel helmets would not be issued for over a year. Individual equipment included a Lee Enfield rifle, back pack, leather pouches, water bottle on the right, haversack on the left, bayonet in frog also on the left, under the haversack.

One of the carpenters who had recently come forward was Arthur Sambrook. His number was 92725, indicating that he was the 45th man to join; his enlistment was recorded in the *Nuneaton Observer's* weekly 'Roll of Honour' on 14 May, along with the names of fifteen other new recruits to the Company. The column reporting these names was headed: 'Avenge the Lusitania! Remember the Verdict – Wilful Murder against the

Emperor of Germany.' Vengeance was probably far from Sambrook's mind when, on 8 May, at the age of seventeen years and six weeks and with two years' experience as a carpenter's apprentice with the building firm of G.E. and W. Wincott (working hours 6 - 5.30 weekdays and 6 - 12 Saturdays), he went along Coton Road to call upon Major MacMullen, be enlisted in the 216th R.E. and, he recalled, receive 'the Woodbine and match that MacMullen presented to every accepted recruit'.

A Woodbine and a match was a poor substitute for the King's shilling, but was perhaps an appropriate induction into a war where tobacco bulked large. For instance, the *Nuneaton Chronicle* had for some months been publicizing a subscription fund for sending out parcels of what it called 'the soothing weed' to the British Army. It explained: 'The French people have been very generous to Tommy Atkins in regard to "Smokes", but Tommy dislikes their cigarettes. He says they have no "bite" in them. He longs for the British "fag".' The *Chronicle* published weekly a list of subscribers, one of whom was Captain Cook, whose five shillings would have provided twenty ounces of pipe tobacco and a hundred 'Kitchener' brand cigarettes. The *Chronicle* also published extracts from an article in *The Lancet* upon the 'psychophysicological' benefits of smoking in allaying 'the restlessness and muscular irritability engendered by mental and physical fatigue'.[12]

Sambrook was sent to the Drill Hall in the Recreation Ground, the Company Headquarters, to see Captain Cook. On his way there he fell in with a friend who had also just enlisted; he was George Harvey (known as 'Dick'), an old Grammar-School boy, son of a local pawnbroker; and the articled pupil of a Nuneaton architect. The two lads were kitted out together with uniforms and equipment, for, though the earliest members of the Company had at first drilled wearing their own clothes, uniforms and kit were now available; these were in the charge of John Wheway, promoted to corporal, as quartermaster. C.S.M. Mitchinson came into the stores while the latest recruits were there and did not like the way they were lounging about, 'judging from his very impolite remarks when he welcomed us to the army'.

The only other N.C.O.s in the Company at that time were two regular R.E. 2nd corporals named Lee and Seymour: their rank was peculiar to the Royal Engineers and was intermediate between lance corporal and corporal. When the Company came to full strength both men were promoted to sergeant, as, too, was Wheway; at the same time a number of sappers became lance corporals. Lee had charge of numbers 1 and 2 sections, constituting the right half-company, and Seymour numbers 3 and 4 sections, constituting the left half-company; there was also a headquarters section, which included company headquarters and (still to arrive) the Company's, mostly horsed, transport. Seymour had been in France in 1914 but was sent home with shell shock. He was said to be 'stout and amiable' and 'a bit of a lad'. A group photograph published in the *Midland Daily Tribune*, miscaptioned '215th Company', portrays Captain Cook, flanked by his four N.C.O.s and 51 of the 60 or more local men who had joined by 14 May, all described as sappers though some, we know, were pioneers or drivers.

The group photograph shows a Sapper William Keen who does not figure in the Nuneaton newspaper 'Rolls of Honour'. Later recruits listed in those rolls down to 11 June are named as: Percy Bailey, William Berry, Fred Bott, John Brunt, Tom Burdett, Cecil Capet, Alf Chamberlain, Mike Cuffe, Dennis Douglas, William Dyer, Fred Earp, George Harris, Isaac Jackson, Samuel Kinsey, George Lago, George Lowndes, Frank Moore, Enderby Parratt, Albert Reynolds, Bill Rogers, Roland Shepherd, Frank E. Smith, Emanuel Taylor, Alf Thomas, Samuel Ward, Arthur Walters, Jack Williams, Walter Woodfield, and Thomas Wright: twenty-seven in four weeks. (Ward and Woodfield would be killed in France.) William Keen, Cuffe, Lago, and Shepherd, like Baxter and Follett before them, came from Tamworth and thus were not strictly local men. Alfred Dodds, the boxer, subject of an anecdote to come, also enlisted, though his name seems not to have been printed in the newspapers.

Sapper Jack Williams's enlistment was remembered by his comrades. The Company was about to march off to attend a military funeral in Nuneaton Parish Church when, as Arthur Daulman recalled, Williams 'appeared on the scene obviously the worse for drink. He had come from the Police Station where he had been to attest, that is, to join up. It was early days and we probably wanted to make a bit of a show, so an angry sergeant-major greeted him menacingly with "I'll see you in the morning". The confrontation took place the following morning, the sergeant-major opening with "We tame lions in the army"; "We eat the buggers where I come from" came the reply. They both came from Brummagem and were never the best of friends after that.' Daulman also recorded the end of Williams's service in the Company about six months later, when they were undergoing engineering training in Buxton. 'One night Spr Jack Williams had been on the beer and came in very noisy indeed. Sgt-Major Mitchinson tried to get him quietly up to his bedroom. On the landing there was a bit of a skirmish and they came through the banisters with Williams on top and his hands around Mitchinson's throat. Well, the guard had to intervene and Williams was given ninety days in Knutsford, a military prison, and transferred to another company. I was to see him about three years later in France on Armistice Day.'

Documents for the enlistment of Frederick Bott on 27 May 1915 survive. He was a stonemason, aged 31, with a wife and four children. He attested before Major MacMullen that he was willing to be vaccinated and to be enlisted for General Service, and he was willing to serve for the duration of the War if His Majesty should so long require his service. He swore that he would bear true Allegiance to His Majesty King George the Fifth, his Heirs and Successors, would, as in duty bound, defend His Majesty against all enemies, and would obey all orders of His Majesty and of the Generals and Officers set over him. Bott's medical examination seems to have been as cursory as Daulman's because the only details recorded were his age, height, expanded chest measurement, range of chest expansion, and 'Scar Left Elbow'. His craft proficiency was examined on 10 June by a local civilian master builder, J.H. Smith in Coton Road, who certified that he was a very good stonemason. Captain Cook enlisted him as a skilled craftsman with the rank of sapper. (He would be wounded in France, repatriated, and demobilized in 1916; the last service record of him is his pension in 1919 for a disability attributable to neurasthenia or `shell-shock'.) Younger, relatively unskilled recruits, such as the apprentices Daulman and Sambrook, were enlisted as pioneers. The weekly pay of a pioneer was 8s.2d. (41 p.) rising to 11s.8d. (58 p.) on completion of recruit training while that of a sapper was 11s.8d. rising to 15s.2d. (76 p.) on completion of recruit training with the possibility of reaching between 17s.6d. (87 p.) and £1 2s.2d. (£1 11p.). However, even a pioneer was wealthier than an infantry of the line private who was paid 7s. (35 p.) on enlistment and from 8s.9d. (44 p.) to 10s.6d. (52 p.) after two years' service. Unsurprisingly there was a rhyme, one version of which reads:

The Lord made men, bees make honey;
The infantry do the work, the R.E.s get the money.

The *Nuneaton Observer* on 28 May 1915 noted a preponderance of married men among recent recruits and complained that the single men of the town were not doing their duty: 'Unless they quickly rally to the Colours they will have justified the title of "slackers"'. On 11 June it put its journalistic weight behind a forthcoming great demonstration in Riversley Park by women who had relatives at the war or in training. 'Rich and poor alike will take part in the event.' It is hoped that this will 'shame the slackers' and persuade them to join up. 'A gigantic British army would strike terror into the Germans.' In the same issue it was able to report that the strength of the 216th (Fortress) Company, R.E., was 86 (exclusive of officers) and that there were vacancies for only sixteen more men: 'Five masons are wanted, and also a harness-maker and a few carpenters'. Two weeks later the Company was still ten men short and Captain Cook made a personal appeal in the newspapers' correspondence columns. He explained that it would be easy to fill these vacancies from other districts, but he wanted local men: 'It would be a sorry task to have to appeal personally to young men to fulfil what is surely a patriotic obligation, and I earnestly hope that this week end will see the Company brought up to full strength by the enlistment of the men we want, viz. Nuneaton men'. As masons were thin on the ground in Nuneaton, he would happily take bricklayers instead. This last push recruited Sappers J. Briddon, C.E. Elsworth, C. Freeman, Harry Holt, R. Poulton, and J.E. Sewell, and Driver F.C. Toogood. (Holt would be killed in France.)

By now Captain Cook had the services of two newly-commissioned second-lieutenants, named Knox and Smith. Kenneth Knox, 31 years old, well-built and over six feet tall, was the son of Jimmy Knox, director of the Haunchwood Brick and Tile Company, who lived in some style in a large house, 'The Chase', on the edge of the town in Higham Lane. At the outbreak of the war Kenneth and his brother Cecil (a future recipient of the Victoria Cross) were working as engineers on railway construction in Alberta; both men came home and enlisted in different companies of Royal Engineers. Four of their brothers were also army officers in the Great War; two of them were killed in action in France. Lieutenant Harry Foster Smith (son of David Smith, a lay chaplain with the Navvy Missionary Society on large public works such as the Manchester Ship Canal) was ten years younger than Kenneth Knox and came to the Nuneaton Company direct from Birmingham University Officer Training Corps. He had entered the University in 1913, from Birmingham Municipal Technical School, and begun a course in Engineering, which he broke off after a year and a half in order to join the army; he was commissioned on 29 May 1915, aged 21. Cook, Knox, and Smith would all go on to win decorations for bravery in the course of the war, though the first two did so having left the 216th for service in R.E. field companies. Lieutenant Harry Foster Smith was the only one of the three to serve with the Nuneaton Company until the end of the war.

For all their importance, the officers of the 216th R.E. do not figure largely in the recollections of their men. The sapper took his orders from and occasionally joked with his section sergeant. Officers belonged to a distinct and different social class. All three officers of the 216th Company would have spent some considerable time away from Nuneaton, receiving technical instruction in military engineering, horsemanship, and drill on short courses at the old R.E. training centre at Chatham or the one newly established at Newark. Even so, the two second lieutenants at first joined the men in the physical training, marching, and drill that were intended to transform a group of civilian craftsmen and apprentices into soldiers. Initial basic military training included such essential skills as saluting, standing to attention, forming a straight line on parade, turning by numbers, and wheeling from line into a column of fours for route marching. These were skills to which many members of the company who had been Boy Scouts (e.g. Frank Adams and Frank Hextall), or members of the Church Lads' Brigade (e.g. Addison, Daulman, Wilf Cox, and the two Fenn brothers) or the Junior Citizens' Training Corps (which Charles Streather helped to set up in Nuneaton) were no strangers. Men with experience of such typical Edwardian embodiments of smartness, good order, discipline, patriotism, and respect for the established social order were put in key positions on the flanks during squad and company drill, which was carried out or muddled through on the recreation ground beside the Drill Hall. Arthur Daulman was struck by the fact that 'much of the drill came from the Boer War experience'.

The local newspapers never tired of praising the smartness of the company in the hands of their 'popular' sergeant-major, but Pioneer Sambrook was not so sure that his comrades came up to scratch. He recalled that C.S.M. Mitchinson 'presided over all these outdoor shows with the idea in his head that we could equal the Guards in smartness and precision, but we never did, no one else wanted to. After six weeks our square bashing was over. We had passed out after a brilliant display and an inspection. I think it was more likely John [C.S.M. Mitchinson] and the two other N.C.O.s were weary of shouting and having to watch our performance. We ourselves were weary of going through such silly evolutions as "At the halt on the left form platoon", carried out from columns of fours. This particularly out-of-date movement was satirized in a part-song popular in canteens and places where they sing. Sung to the tune of "Three Cheers for the Red White and Blue", it went: "At the halt on the left form platoon, At the halt, etc., If the odd numbers don't mark time two paces, How the hell can the rest form platoon." In our case, if the even numbers and the right flank came round running we made some sort of a show. Actually, apart from forming fours, about turning, turning right and left, this platoon business was our best performance; the other evolutions in Caesar's drill manual had to be seen to be believed, and even John could not believe while he was watching them.'

He also recalls: 'Sometimes we were lectured by Mitch on the behaviour and smartness expected from a crack corps, but on looking round on the ill-fitting khaki uniforms we wore his exhortation did not carry much weight. As these lectures went on we began to wonder if we were in the Household Cavalry instead of the Royal Engineers. The only degree of smartness we could practise was brought about by the use of a button stick and polish on buttons and cap badge.' In the matter of personal smartness the veterans of the Church Lads' Brigade had an advantage of course. Pioneer Daulman 'never had any trouble, for example, putting on puttees and arranging them smartly, as some did'. He 'had done it so often before. The trick was to put a half twist in the puttee which prevented a loop in the back. To pull them tight was to invite varicose veins,' he recalled.

Physical training, including exercises on the vaulting horse, and varied sometimes by a three-mile run, was supervized by C.S.M. Mitchinson. There were regular bathing parades to the Corporation swimming baths. The War Office manual of Royal Engineer training stipulated that 'manly games are of value', especially if 'so arranged that all, and not only selected teams, take their part'.[13] This was the principle enshrined in C.S.M Mitchinson's speciality, the boxing parade. Sambrook recalled that 'the company was formed up in two equal ranks, facing inwards. John produced two pairs of boxing gloves, which were donned by the first opposite chaps and then they sparred and punched for three minutes, and so on until everyone had taken his turn. Any man who in John's opinion was not making a proper effort, he took on himself for three minutes. Such a case occurred in the match Dodds v "Cubby" Marston. Dodds was an amateur middleweight of some local renown, about 25 years of age. Cubby was 48 years old and had no idea of punching anyone. Dodds just sparred round and contented himself with tapping Cubby's gloves. Cubby thought that was real boxing and did the same until John in disgust bellowed out "Get stuck into each other you pair of cripples" and stopped the round, saying "I'll show you what boxing is, Dodds". When John put on Cubby's gloves the rest of us began to take some interest. The round started by John putting his face forward, dancing about from side to side, and saying "See if you can hit that Dodds". This was John's usual technique, moving his head out of the way, and evading his opponent's blows. "Easy", replied Dodds: "How's that?", delivering a punch which made the sergeant-major wipe his nose. "That's luck", said John and held his face out again. "That's asking for it", replied Dodds, connecting with another hefty punch, and then they both set to in earnest. John got a good dusting. When the bout was ended Mitch said "I see what you mean Dodds". Thereafter the boxing gloves seem to have been mislaid and we had no more boxing sessions.'

The sergeant-major also sportingly turned out for the cricket eleven captained by Sapper Streather. One day, combining business with pleasure, the company route-marched to the Butts ground in Coventry for the cricket team to play the local Coventry Royal Engineers company, and then marched back. The 216th R.E. cricketers were good enough to defeat all local Nuneaton competition and win the F.C. Payne cup, but met more than their match when Gilbert Jessop, the England and Gloucestershire player (famed for scoring the fastest ever first-class century) brought to Nuneaton a side drawn from his battalion of the Manchester Regiment, then stationed at Lichfield. The Nuneaton company were all out for 44 (Jessop 7 for 23); the Manchesters passed this total for the loss of one wicket and then went on to make 215 for 8. Jessop scored 68 in next to no time before being caught at deep cover by Charlie Streather, as reported by the *Nuneaton Observer*: 'the old Grammar School boy doing a little somersault, evidently proud of the honour in bringing about the downfall of one of England's greatest cricketers'.[14] Jessop's side consisted almost entirely of officers, including a lieutenant-colonel. There were no officers in the 216 R.E.'s eleven. The Gentlemen beat the (sort of) Players.

All through their initial training in Nuneaton the local men lived each day partly under military discipline and partly at home, as if civilians. This was the general case with locally raised units: it was an expedient forced upon a War Office which did not have enough camps to cope with the flood of volunteers to an unprecedentedly large army, but it had the valuable side effect of giving the local community a visible share in a common patriotic duty. On a typical day the newly-enlisted sapper might report to the Drill Hall at 0700 hours in canvas shoes for P.T. until 0830, go home for breakfast, come back on parade to spend the rest of the morning on squad and company drill and general infantry training, go home for dinner, come back for afternoon exercises in a range of skills from the judging of distances outdoors, when dry, to the tying of knots indoors, when wet, then home for tea. For meals at home there was a ration allowance of 1s.2d. a day (i.e. nearly 6p). In the later stages of training there were route marches, progressively increasing from five or six miles to twelve or thirteen, and eventually more than twenty. The company also learned the all-important skill of trench-digging, though not in quite the conditions they were to experience in France. They spent hours in front of the parapets, lifting turfs from the ground in front to mask the earth dug and thrown out of the trench while their officers went up the slope facing to see if these defences were concealed. The *Nuneaton Chronicle* of 6 August tells us more of these earthworks, which were laid out on five acres in The Slang[15], near Haunchwood Brick Works, which were made available by Lieutenant Knox's father and were 'supposed to be dominated by an enemy advancing from Camp Hill'. These trenches, *Chronicle* readers were told, 'were planned on the actual models used at the memorable Battle of the Aisne, and constituted splendid examples of skill, the works including a redoubt, machine-gun emplacements, and every detail made familiar to present-day readers of newspapers.' We can be sure they were full-sized too, because the Engineer Training manual declared sternly: 'The making of works on reduced scales is forbidden'.[16]

In all these activities the civilian world was very close. Nuneaton townsfolk turned out to watch their sons, husbands, and fathers carrying out their drill and physical jerks on the recreation ground, and on fine Sunday evenings they inspected and admired the trenches at Haunchwood. When the Company was fallen out for a breather during drill the older men would go to the Nag's Head, the nearest pub to the recreation ground, for a pint, while the youngsters (such as Pioneers Daulman, Hextall, and Sambrook) would repair to a café on the corner of Queen's Road (where Clarke's the greengrocer stood later) for a glass of pop with a dollop of ice-cream in it.

The proximity of public houses imposed problems of discipline. Arthur Daulman recalled an episode very early in the Company's history, when C.S.M. Mitchinson was their only N.C.O.: 'It was Saturday morning and we were on parade on the rec. when Joe Webster, bricklayer, and George Harris, plasterer, appeared in a very merry state. They had been detailed to squeezee the Drill Hall but had gone off leaving their tunics and caps behind. At this time public houses were open all day and they found their way to the Coach and Horses. In this dishevelled state they appeared to the amusement and anticipation of most of us. "Fall in two men" was the order and the culprits were marched to the clink. The

recreational outlets, in the form of clubs and concerts etc. and why public houses in Rugby were obliged to stop serving drinks at 9.30 p.m. However, drunken behaviour appears not to have found much coverage in the *Advertiser*, perhaps in the interests of public relations, or perhaps because the problem in the town was insignificant. In the billeting area as a whole, there were some complaints by soldiers about unsatisfactory accommodation or food, although, again, these do not appear to have been voiced in the Rugby paper, presumably for the reasons stated above. Overall, the behaviour of the soldiers during their time in Rugby was praised by local people, as it was in most of the Divisional billeting area.

Traditionally, sport was an important part of regimental life and its importance to the physical fitness of soldiers recognised by their senior officers. The arrival of the soldiers in the Warwickshire area temporarily revitalised sport, which had declined following the enlistment in the forces of so many local young men. In Rugby, the town's Football Club soon placed their ground at the disposal of the troops for football and other games. This was in response to a request from Captain Lucas.[9] Both the Royal Inniskilling Fusiliers and the King's Own Scottish Borderers were reported to have good Association football teams and the battalions entered teams for the annual Rugby Hospital Cup. On 31st January, the Border Regiment beat Rugby F.C. 5-1 in the first semi-final, the game being watched by 2,000 spectators. A few days later, in the second semi-final, the Royal Inniskilling Fusiliers defeated a K.O.S.B. team 4-0. When the Fusiliers went on to win the Hospital Cup, beating the Border regiment 3-0, the game was watched by between 2,000 and 3,000 people. Proceeds from the competiton went to St Cross Hospital, the local division of the St John's Ambulance Brigade and to the Rugby District Nursing Association.

The soldiers enjoyed rather less success in their games of Rugby football, with teams from each regiment being defeated by Rugby School, and the King's Own Scottish Borderers losing to a Rugby and District team. Other sporting fixtures included hockey, Rink hockey, in which roller skates were used, and boxing tournaments. On 9th February, a Grand Military Boxing Tournament was announced, to be held at the Rugby Rink on 11th and 12th February. Ticket prices ranged from 1s to 4s, with soldiers in uniform admitted to the 1s seats at half price. Proceeds went to the Belgian Relief Fund and the winners were to be presented with a silver cup, valued at £10 10s. In the event, the Tournament was won by the Border Regiment, helped by Drummer Crone, champion light-weight boxer of India. St Matthews Boys' School was one of the schools providing entertainment at the tournament, in the form of songs and dances. A second tournament was held in March.

Not all of the intended sporting fixtures went to plan. In January, the famous Birchfield Harriers came to Rugby to run against a team of soldiers. Unfortunately, "none of the soldiers turned out, thus robbing the event of much of its interest". Several members of the British Thomson-Houston (B.T.H.) Harriers turned out but "failed to make much of a show" on the 6 mile course, though the *Rugby Advertiser* did point out that very few runners were now left in the district, as practically all of them had joined up.[10] However, in early February, teams from the Border Regiment and Royal Inniskilling Fusiliers did take part in a cross country run, along with an VIII from Rugby School; the School emerged triumphant.

As soon as the soldiers were settled, training got under way. Large scale manoeuvres at brigade or divisional level were constrained by the widespread dispersal of the soldiers in the area and by the nature of the local countryside, with its small, enclosed fields. Training at company and battalion level did proceed. Given that the Division's regular soldiers already possessed most of the necessary martial skills, the main emphasis appears to have been placed on improving the soldiers' levels of fitness. Within four days of their arrival, route marches were being undertaken, the soldiers being preceded, during the day at least, by their regimental bands. Troops also marched at night, motorists being warned to be aware of their possible presence. Route marches also gave an opportunity for the Division's transport to be tested, as well as such items as field kitchens. There were daily company exercises and the soldiers also practised trench digging. A Divisional bomb-making and explosives 'school' was established near Rugby and this was attended by officers who could practise their newly developed skills on bits of railway line, trenches and wire entanglements. Lieutenant Guy Nightingale, of the 1st Battalion Royal Munster Fusiliers, who journeyed from Coventry to attend a course, found it all "very dangerous" and throwing grenades at night "more dangerous still". He seemed quite relieved that, on the course he attended, only one casualty, an officer from the Royal Inniskilling Fusiliers, was sustained.[11]

As the time for departure approached, so the battalions and other units were brought together in their respective brigades, with each brigade managing one combined exercise. In the case of the 87th Brigade, this was held on 4th March at Bilton Grange.

The war diaries for the units accommodated in Rugby generally start with the departure of these units overseas. One exception was the 87th Field Ambulance of the RAMC, for which the diary for March 1915 survives. Although a Territorial unit (originally the 1st West Lancashire Field Ambulance), which was mobilised in the Divisional area, its diary gives some insight into the work being carried out during its stay in Rugby. Each day, apart from Sunday, began early for the men, with a parade at 7.15 a.m., followed by a second parade at 9.30 a.m. Mornings were usually occupied with drill or short route marches, or with practices, such as packing the unit's wagons. Afternoons might be given over to lectures. Equipment had to be overhauled and consignments of blankets, saddlery, harnesses etc had to be assimilated. In the middle of the month, 73 mules were received. Fresh details of men from the Reserve were taken on to the strength, in order to replace those deemed unfit for overseas service. At the Brigade exercise on 4th March, the unit practised establishing and equipping a dressing station and collecting wounded by night. The local Voluntary Aid Detachment (VAD) Hospital was used for the exercise as a Casualty Clearing Station (CCS) and the chain of treatment and the evacuation of the wounded was completed by using borrowed motor vehicles to take 'wounded' men from the CCS to rail heads at Rugby. For a while, the unit's officers also took medical charge of the VAD Hospital at Ashlawn, although it is not clear whether this was done in order to improve medical care at the Hospital or to give the officers relevant experience.

The Hospital at Ashlawn, which was run by the Hillmorton and Ashlawn VADs, had been opened in January on the instructions of the War office so as to provide for the needs of the billeted troops. It contained 27 beds and furniture to equip it was lent by local people. By the time the troops left, just over 100 cases had been dealt with at the Hospital, with more than 90% of the patients discharged for duty.[12]

Nor was the men's spiritual welfare neglected and each Sunday began with church parade. Services for Anglicans, Catholics, Presbyterians, as well as members of other churches, such as Wesleyans, were held in the town. The intense local interest in the soldiers is reflected in the large numbers of people who turned out to watch the troops march to and from the churches, led by their bands. The *Rugby Advertiser* reported "dense crowds" outside the Parish Church on 18th January and "several thousand" on the 25th. For many soldiers, of course, church parade was something that they had to accept, however unenthusiastically. Oswin Creighton, newly appointed Chaplain to the 86th Infantry Brigade said of his experiences with soldiers billeted in Nuneaton: "I find them very nice, very civil and easy to talk to. But I feel quite at sea as to how to do any direct religious work with them."[13] However, some were more devout and entered into the spiritual life of the local communities in which they now found themselves. One was Serjeant James Johnston, of the 1st Battalion Border Regiment, who quickly immersed himself in the life of the local Baptist community. A 29 year-old regular soldier from Cumberland, he contacted the

Rugby Baptist Church through the 'welcome club' at the Baptist Schoolroom. "He lived for spiritual things. ... His faith was his dominant passion", said Pastor J.H. Lees. During his time in Rugby, he gave talks at the Baptist Church, including "quite the best missionary address we have ever had", as well as conducting services at the Baptist Chapels at Dunchurch and Draycote, and at the Rugby Railway Mission. An enthusiastic advocate of temperance, he was reported as "having induced many men in the Regiment to sign the total abstinence pledge".[14] It seems that his wife, Mary, joined him at Rugby and participated in his religious work.

Other soldiers contributed to sustaining the work of the Home Mission. Sergeant Mudd, of the Royal Inniskilling Fusiliers, gave an address to the Mission's annual meeting, held at the Wesleyan Church in January. He explained the Christian work among soldiers in His Majesty's Army. Representatives of the Lodge of Good Templars, connected with the Royal Inniskilling Fusiliers, provided vocal accompaniment at the meeting, including a solo, "Our God is marching on", sung by Private Miller. The Military Good Templar Lodge held meetings at the Co-operative Hall during their stay in Rugby, including dances and concerts. The YMCA Recreation Rooms were also used by soldiers with a view to inculcating the habits of temperance, thrift and an aversion to gambling.

Two of the Division's soldiers never left Rugby. On 8th March, Private James Macdonald of the King's Own Scottish Borderers died at Ashlawn Red Cross Hospital in the town. He had been admitted 24 hours previously and had been assessed by medical officers of the 87th Field Ambulance. The peculiar smell of the man's breath suggested diabetes, and this was confirmed by examination of a urine sample. Unfortunately, the coma into which Private Macdonald had slipped deepened and he died the following morning. The cause of death was confirmed as diabetes. James Macdonald was 23 years old and came from Glasgow. His mother travelled to Warwickshire for the funeral, as did one of his brothers who was recovering from wounds received whilst serving with the BEF. Another three brothers were also in the army. Private Macdonald was buried with full military honours and large numbers of local people, as well as many soldiers, lined the route taken by the cortege to the cemetery in Clifton Road. A firing party fired three volleys at the graveside and pipers and drummers from his regiment played 'Loch Habberd no more'. The ceremony was "one of the most unique of its kind ever seen in Rugby".[15]

Equally unfortunate was 26 year old Private Stewart Gardner of the Royal Inniskilling Fusiliers, who died on 31st March. He had just returned to his lodgings from a spell in hospital with pneumonia. He was looking forward to a month's furlough and had arranged a rail pass at the local station. After dinner, he sat talking with his landlady before asking if he might go to his bedroom to collect his belongings. Unfortunately, having done so, he fell down the stairs and fractured his skull. He never regained consciousness and died the same evening in hospital. The inquest found that Gardner was sober at the time of the accident but described the stairs as "steep and dark", with an initial "drop step", about which he may simply have forgotten during his time away from the house. Although a number of his family came from Belfast, there was to be no military funeral for Private Gardner – his Battalion had already left the town and had arrived at Alexandria, in Egypt, by the time he was buried in Clifton Road Cemetery.[16]

In early March, there was some movement of units within the billeting area, aimed at a more central concentration of the Division's forces. This was prior to the King's inspection of the Division on 12th March and the departure of the Division for service overseas (a process that began on 15th March). Several battalions changed their billets on 5th and 6th March, with the 1st Essex and 4th Worcesters leaving Banbury for Warwick and Leamington, the 2nd Hampshires leaving Stratford for Warwick, the 1st Royal Dublin Fusiliers leaving Nuneaton for Kenilworth and the 2nd Royal Fusiliers moving from Stockingford to Coventry. To make room for the Royal Fusiliers in Coventry, the 2nd South Wales Borderers moved from the city to Rugby on 5th March, thus completing the concentration of the 87th Brigade in the town. (The Borderers were billeted at New Bilton, on the outskirts of Rugby, some consolation for those who felt they had been overlooked in the original billeting arrangements.) Finally, on 8th March, the 1/5th Royal Scots journeyed from Scotland to Leamington, thereby providing the Division's final infantry battalion.

On the morning of 12th March, the Division's twelve infantry battalions, along with the Divisional artillery brigades located in the area and "representative parties of other units", assembled along the London Road between its intersection with the Fosse Way and the railway station at Dunchurch. They were drawn up in a line, some two miles long, on the broad verge on the northern side of the road. The infantry lined up four deep. There they waited for the arrival of King George V and his staff. It was mid-morning that the royal party drew into Dunchurch station and mounted the horses that were waiting for them. On leaving the station, George V and his entourage rode slowly down the ranks of soldiers, who came to attention as the King approached. As each regiment passed, its colonel walked by the King's side down the line of troops.

The King reached the crossroads, where the London Road and Fosse Way intersect, at about 12.15 p.m. and took up a position on the south-west corner. "Then the march past commenced, the artillery in column of route, followed by the infantry in double fours (eight abreast). ... Twelve splendid battalions, each at war strength in personnel, with fixed bayonets, filling the broad roadway from edge to edge and constantly flowing onwards under the canopy of gigantic elm trees, was a splendid spectacle ..."[17] The King returned the salute of every officer and a regimental band played as the troops moved past. As they got clear of the saluting point, units returned, by pre-arranged routes, to their billeting areas.

The four battalions that made up the 87th Brigade would have had a relatively short march from Rugby to the inspection point, where they would have taken up a position between the 86th and 88th Brigades. Within the Brigade, battalions would have been ordered according to seniority: South Wales Borderers, Kings Own Scottish Borderers, Royal Inniskilling Fusiliers and Border Regiment. The role of the 87th Field Ambulance, also billeted at Rugby, was more modest: they provided a stretcher party and an ambulance wagon, under Captain Taylor, which was located at the Blue Boar Inn, in order to deal with any emergencies. The rest of the men continued their duties in Rugby. However, the stretcher party were presumably the RAMC men who treated a military policeman who was thrown from his horse before the review took place. His broken leg was placed in splints and he was removed to hospital.

The date and location of the inspection were not published in advance, although the event was widely anticipated in the area. Civilian and military police blocked both ends of the London Road, beyond the line of review, as well as access roads. Local people, therefore, had some difficulty in witnessing the event. Nonetheless, the preparations being made by the troops for the occasion alerted many to what was intended and some correctly guessed the location, although others made their way to Stoneleigh Park, in the belief that it would be the assembly point. Some who came from Rugby simply took to the fields flanking the London Road and made their way to the crossroads. Henry Wilkins, a journalist from Coventry, estimated that a crowd of between 1,000 and 1,200 gathered at the saluting place.[18]

The departure of the 29th Division from the area began on 15th March. For a long time it had been assumed that the Division would follow the other Regular Army divisions to the Western Front. The YMCA in Rugby had even been offering soldiers lessons in French, "which should prove of great value to them when they remove to the seat of war".[19] In fact, a struggle for the services of the 29th Division had been taking place, only settled on 10th March, when Lord Kitchener, Secretary of State for War, finally – and reluctantly – decided that the Division would join the Mediterranean Expeditionary Force

1916, there was an appeal for volunteers to train as nurses to allow for further expansion of the hospital, and as a result, the *Stratford Herald* announced:

> Mr and Mrs Fielden have provided rooms at Kineton House, and an additional 15 beds are available, making 50. It is excellent for so small a place as Kineton.[12]

By March of the following year even greater demand produced yet another response in Kineton.

> Mrs Fielden is putting 32 beds in the large dining room of Kineton House. She is giving up her sitting room for the surgery, the schoolroom is to be utilised as a sitting room for the soldiers, and two bedrooms will also be used. The additional accommodation will be ready in the course of a week, and the Red Cross hospital will then accommodate 100. The racquet room will be used as a dining room, and it will be in the charge of a sister and a VAD nurse. The household staff will assist in the remainder of the work. A more delightful place could not be found for a hospital.[13]

The hospital accommodation remained at this level until it finally closed on 21st December 1918.

Discipline

Although the Red Cross in some areas issued figures for average stays of the patients in their VAD hospitals (usually around 40 days), no figures for Kineton – or even Warwickshire – appear to have survived. Little mention is made of the severity of injuries the nurses had to treat. Many of the patients were suffering from shell shock, and from photographs it is clear that others had lost limbs or had been blinded. Much is made of the entertainment and welcome given locally to the in-patients, and this would have been a valuable therapy in overcoming the horrors that the patients had experienced at the front.

The freedom given to them undoubtedly led to problems of discipline, and one misdemeanour in 1915 resulted in a court appearance at Kineton petty sessions, at which arrangements at the hospital were scrutinised. One of the soldiers had eluded his escort while out on a walk, and taken the opportunity to get drunk. None of the Kineton landlords would admit to selling him beer – he had apparently persuaded a third party to buy his drinks – and this third party, a groom, William Bishop of Combroke, was summoned that he "being a person on the licensed premises of the Swan Inn, Kineton, did procure certain intoxicating liquor, to wit, one pint of beer, for consumption by a drunken person, Private Frank Williams, 2nd Cheshire Regiment, on September 2nd". On his return to Clarendon House, the soldier "created a disturbance on the wards for nearly three hours after he got back". The magistrates, chaired on this occasion by Mr Ernest Parke of Moorlands Farm, Butlers Marston, decided that Bishop was guilty, but before they passed sentence, Lady Willoughby de Broke, appearing in her position as Commandant of the hospital, asked that the case should be dealt with severely, because:

> It was a real danger – in some cases almost to life – to soldiers. For one thing it incited them to break away from their escort. Again – and this was a more serious matter – many of these men entered the Hospital with septic wounds, head injuries, brain injuries and so forth, and alcohol might exercise an incalculable amount of bodily harm while they were in this condition. People were making their work at the Hospital much more difficult by encouraging men to break away from their escort, and her Ladyship would be grateful if the bench could make any reference as to this for the welfare of the wounded. Men who got into trouble were, like Williams, sent back to Birmingham in disgrace and put in a solitary ward, and it was one of the most cruel things the public could do to treat them in a manner such as Williams had been treated.[14]

After such a plea by so eminent a person, the bench was not lenient. The groom was fined 40 shillings, and had to pay the expenses of the witnesses attending court, at a time when few workers earned much more than £1 per week.[15] The bench also gave a clear warning that any future cases of this kind would meet with a prison sentence.

Despite this case of drunkenness, it seems reasonable to assume that discipline at the hospital was well handled. There is no evidence whatsoever in the Kineton parish registers that the close proximity of the community of young soldiers with the young nurses and village girls had any effect on the birthrate, illegitimate or otherwise. Temptation must, however, have been on the minds of those in command at the hospital. In January 1916, some Kineton parishioners were firmly rebuked in the pages of the parish magazine:

> May we appeal to a small and thoughtless section of our community? A small number of girls in Kineton are making the lot of those responsible for our wounded a very hard one. Their practice is to go out and waylay the men who go for walks. To be friendly and pass the time of day is one thing, to waylay and hinder escorts doing their duty is another. Such conduct shows a lamentable want of self-respect; those who practice it would be astonished at the strong feeling at the hospital and among the patients and other respectable members of our community, yes, and among the men themselves.[16]

Entertaining the wounded

The majority of soldiers, though, seem to have enjoyed their stay in Kineton's hospital, and, even if romance was discouraged, almost every imaginable entertainment was laid on for them.

There were outings:

> The motor rides and many invitations are greatly appreciated by the soldiers. Last week they were invited to Farnborough Hall where they had a splendid time. On Tuesday Mr A Motion of Upton House kindly entertained them, and they landed some fine fish.[17]

> They have been to Compton Wynyates and the Round House where Mrs Gaskell of Diana Lodge kindly provided the tea. After a further run to Leamington they returned. They have also been to Avon Dassett – to Bitham House and Avon Carrow.[18]

> The round of visiting continues. On Friday, the soldiers attended a conjuring show at the new schools, and tea in the Church rooms. On Saturday there was a concert at Kineton House. On Thursday they went to Stratford-on-Avon to the Christmas tree, and on Saturday and Sunday, Mrs Brand invited them to whist drives and tea. On Monday they gave a concert.[19]

There were Whist Drives in winter and cricket in summer:

> On Tuesday afternoon the wounded of Kineton Hospital played the medical officer and staff, the match being witnessed by a large number of spectators. Excitement was aroused when the Honourable Mabel Verney and Dr Elkington went to the wickets, and a very good game followed. The staff scored 63 in two innings, and the patients 65. Miss Carter bowled well. Mrs Gaskell entertained the teams to tea on the ground which they hugely appreciated.[20]

There were concerts, certainly every two weeks, given by Kineton people for the soldiers, and others in which the soldiers entertained their hosts. A series of these concerts took place after the opening of the "Garland Hall", which was a hut in the grounds of Clarendon House donated by the wealthy American banker, Charles Garland, of Moreton Morrell Hall, and fully fitted out with gas lighting and a billiard table. The hut, which was moved to the sports field in Kineton at the end of the war, can still be seen there today in use as a cricket pavilion. All the concerts included singing and sketches, some dancing – "morris dancing by the National School girls"[21] – others conjuring. One concert given by the soldiers was so well received that they repeated it in the Public Hall, and raised £15 for gramophones for the hospital.[22] The *Stratford Herald* details many programmes, most of which contain popular songs of the day, many now forgotten. The concert given on Monday, 8th January, 1917 is typical.

> In the concert given that evening the songs were all well rendered. Messrs. Chandler and Garrett also contributed comic songs which were, as usual, warmly received. One patient's song in particular was loudly applauded. *"If I could only make you care"* by Private H Hutchinson of the 1st Leicesters, who though he has recently had the misfortune to lose a leg while serving his country, sets a grand example of heroism by his cheerfulness and bravery in his trouble. A sketch specially written for the occasion by Private Porter was well acted and somewhat diverting, the fun arising out of an advertisement for a suitable wife. Justice was done to the respective characters, and the piece seemed to be generally enjoyed.

The programme that evening also contained songs from the hospital sister, songs from five of the soldier-patients, and ended with the national anthem.[23]

Hospital financing

In 1917 the British Red Cross formulated regulations to govern the employment of nursing VADs in military hospitals. Volunteers were required to be between 21 and 48 years of age for home service and 23 and 42 for overseas. After one month on probation, the matron assessed their suitability, and if all was satisfactory they were then required to sign an agreement to serve for six months or the duration of the war, at home or abroad. They were to be paid £20 per annum, with increments of £2 10s 0d every six months up to a maximum of £30 per annum. It was also laid down that VADs should work under fully trained nurses with duties including sweeping, dusting, polishing, cleaning, washing patients' crockery, sorting linen and any nursing duties allotted by the matron. Hospitals received a mere three shillings a day per patient from the War Office, and any further expenditure had to be met by fund-raising.[24]

Whatever the everyday cost of running the hospital, financing the varied entertainments offered must also have been demanding. For the first six months, the hospital was financed by public subscription with Lady Willoughby de Broke and Mrs Fielden acting as guarantors to cover any deficit.[25] There are constant reports of money raising activities both for the Red Cross movement and for the hospital in Kineton. In the churchwarden's receipts are several signed "Dora Fielden, Commandant" for sums of money from the Church collection plate and from the takings at organ recitals, sums varying from 12s 10d to £8 8s 0d. Entertainments were often generously given in aid of the hospital funds by groups from outside the village, though the Kineton audience still had to dig deep for their admission tickets. One such event had tickets at 5s 0d numbered and reserved, 2s 0d reserved, and 1s 0d or 6d unreserved, at a time when a performance in January 1917 at the Shakespeare Theatre in Stratford-upon-Avon cost 5s 3d for the best front row seats, 3s 9d for the stalls and 7d for the cheapest gallery seats. It was given by the Army Pay Corps, and included a choir of 40 men, humorous items, glees, pianoforte solos and elocutionists, and raised £26 10s 0d.[26] Another took place in May 1917 when the Kineton Choral Society invited Shipston Choral Society to give a performance of *"The Messiah"* in St Peter's. It resulted in a profit of £21 10s 0d for the hospital.

Summer fetes

All these fund raising activities, useful as they undoubtedly were, pale into insignificance when compared to the fund raising fetes held in the summers of 1916 and 1917. The fetes were well advertised and planned. Visitors to the first wartime fete in Kineton were promised the opportunity of meeting Captain Bruce Bairnsfather, a Royal Warwickshire Regiment man, best remembered for humorous war cartoons in *"The Bystander"* involving the character called "Old Bill". They were promised countless other attractions, all on the August Bank Holiday that had been officially cancelled because of the war. The people of Warwickshire appear not to have noticed, and poured into Kineton on foot, by bicycle, and by special train.

> The pretty grounds of Kineton House (kindly lent by Mr J Fielden) presented an animated and picturesque scene on Monday last, the occasion being a garden fete organised in aid of the Clarendon Red Cross Hospital and War Supply depot. An extensive programme containing a variety of items had been prepared by willing helpers and, favoured by the weather, which could not have been better, the fete proved a big success. Among the numerous attractions offered were concerts, a dramatic sketch, sports, competitions, a Punch-and-Judy show for the entertainment of the children, a palmist etc., while delightful selections were given throughout the afternoon by the Stratford-on-Avon band under the able conductorship of Mr J Cheney. An exhibition of needlework was on show and for sale in the hall, as was a doll's house, the work of Miss Webb's pupils, the models for which were made by Master Fred Griffin, while in the grounds was to be seen a very efficiently furnished first-aid dressing station, erected by Dr Price and Mr Webb. Stalls of all descriptions, and refreshments were dotted here and there in the grounds ... and the wounded soldiers who were present gave their aid wherever it was needed.

Two well attended concerts were given in the drawing room of Kineton House during the day, presided over by Mr Guernsey Walsingham Webb at the piano.

> The chief item in the programme, that by Captain Bruce Bairnsfather, the popular war cartoonist, was reserved to last. ... Welcoming him, Mr Webb said the Kineton audience all knew that at the commencement of war, Captain Bairnsfather joined up and went to France: he was blown up, had shell-shock, and came back to England. He returned to France and was at the front at the beginning of the great push which was going on now, but not having fully recovered from the shock he had to come home again on sick-leave. Captain Bairnsfather, who appeared by special permission of *The Bystander*, then delighted his audience with two of his irresistible lightning sketches, showing the humorous side of life in the trenches: "Ere it is again" and "Watchman, what of the night". Another sketch "A Hopeless Dawn" drawn previous to the concert was also given by the artist. Immediately after these had been passed round for those present to inspect, they were taken outside and sold by auction, where in about ten minutes they had raised the handsome sum of £85.[27]

Afternoon sports were followed by dancing, and, as reported a week later, the sum of £468 14s 8d had been raised.

The 1916 fete was but a preamble to the one held in 1917. In that year the farmers of the area formed a large committee to organise the event, and brought money and new ideas for fund-raising. They invited Miss Mary Anderson, an American actress then living in Broadway, Worcestershire, to open the fete. She was undoubtedly a charismatic figure who had achieved great popularity because of her exceptional beauty, and who, despite her 57 years of age, had just played Juliet in the balcony scene of *Romeo and Juliet* at the London Coliseum.[28] At the concert held at the fete in a huge marquee on the lawn, she recited Lawrence Binyon's poem that is now so well known.

> "They shall grow not old
> As we that are left grow old;
> Age shall not weary them nor years condemn:
> On the going down of the sun and in the morning
> We will remember them."

In the evening there was a cinema show, and events ended with an auction of gifts donated by the farmers of the neighbourhood. The auction even included a pedigree bull calf presented by Mr Ernest Parke of Moorlands Farm. The result of this massive effort was a sum of £700 for the hospital, and the *Stratford Herald* of 17th August 1917 carried an editorial to mark the success.

> THE KINETON FETE
>
> The most sanguine supporter of this movement could scarcely have expected so splendid a result. But it was well deserved. Everything was admirably conceived, intelligently carried out, and the event took a shape that brought entertainment to a vast number of people. Few expected that from *five to six thousand* [my italics] people would find their way to the little Warwickshire town now so bereft of Railway accommodation. Had some accurate knowledge of the crowd been formed more bountiful provision would have been made for their personal requirements. The Food Controller, had he been present, would have had an experience that would have been useful to him in his future onerous and not very thankful task. Refreshments were decidedly scarce, and teas had, perforce, to take a rational turn. Many tried the purveyors of the little town to supply their wants, but one and all had gone to the fete, shut up shop, and despised business for the day. Much more money might have been made in the purveying department had there been the slightest premonition of so vast a crowd. But few complaints were forthcoming. Everyone was attracted by a noble cause, and cared little for disappointments of this kind. The result was grand – a sum of £700 for the VA Hospital! The money is wanted. It is an institution that has restored to health and strength many scores of our brave Tommies, and it will continue its fine work while so many generous and patriotic people take a keen interest in its usefulness and efficiency.[29]

With such accolades being heaped upon the village it is perhaps not surprising that the two commandants who had done so much for the hospital both received Honours in 1918. Mrs Dora Fielden was given the OBE in the New Year's Honours List, and Lady Willoughby de Broke the same honour in the Birthday Honours, a little later that year.

The end of the War and a death at the hospital

As the year and the war dragged on, the VAD Hospital continued to treat and entertain patients in the same sort of way. On 11th November, the Armistice was signed, and:

> The inmates of the hospitals have been especially jubilant this week, and all kinds of amusements have been entered into in honour of the cessation of hostilities.[30]

Then, suddenly, three days later, disaster struck. One of the patients, Corporal Horace Thomas, died. It would appear he was the only patient out of the 2168 wounded who were treated there to die in Kineton. Once again affairs at the hospital were scrutinised in court, and the story of a sad accident came out. Corporal Thomas was a twenty-year old who had been admitted to Clarendon Hospital suffering from shell-shock, and from attacks of giddiness. One evening, when helping to get seats through a trap door into the dining room, for one of the famous concerts, it seems he slipped and fell, knocking his head. He never regained consciousness. The nurse, a local girl, had been fetching him some clean collars for the concert, but she was exonerated from blame, and the coroner pronounced himself satisfied that it had been an accident.[31] Nevertheless it must have come as a severe blow to the staff of the hospital, and the people of Kineton honoured him as best they could when his coffin was taken to the station for burial at his home in London.

> The greatest respect was shown on Tuesday, when the body was taken from the hospital to the station en route for London, blinds being drawn both at the Hospitals and at private houses. The cortège was headed by the Commandant and the sisters and nurses from the Hospitals, while the bier, which contained the remains, was covered with the Union Jack, and upon it rested the deceased's cap. All the soldiers from the Hospitals followed, carrying wreaths. During the latter portion of the journey the coffin was raised shoulder high by six of the deceased's comrades, and, as it reached the station, the rest of the soldiers formed a guard of honour, standing at the salute. Floral tributes were sent by the Commandant (Mrs Fielden), Section staff and men, Q.M. The Hon Mabel Verney, Clarendon staff and men, Kineton House staff and men, etc.[32]

The hospital closed down for Christmas 1918 on 21st December, and never reopened.

Honours for the hospital team

All 200 of the hospital staff, the patients, and those who had in any way helped with the work of caring for the wounded, including sisters, laundry workers, and orderlies, were entertained in the Public Hall to refreshments, cigars and cigarettes, by Mrs Fielden and her team at the beginning of 1919. In September 1919 many of the hospital staff received certificates signed by Queen Alexandra in recognition of their work.[33]

The certificates were presented at a function organised to mark the closure of the VAD Hospitals in Kineton. Those present were addressed by Lady Willoughby de Broke, who, as well as thanking everyone for their sterling effort during the war, exhorted them all to continue with their valuable Red Cross work. The editorial in the *Stratford Herald* echoes her praises.

> 'Well done, Kineton Division!' These words with which Lady Willoughby de Broke concluded her admirable address yesterday form a fitting commentary on the War Record of this pretty Warwickshire town. Situated in the centre of England, it has given from its heart men to fight by land, sea, and air; money to provide the sinews of war, and women who have thrown themselves whole-heartedly into the task of nursing our wounded heroes back to health.[34]

Mrs Fielden then thanked all who had worked at the hospital during the war, mentioning particularly the doctors and the Quartermasters who had taken charge of 110 or so people so well. She concluded by reading highly appreciative letters of thanks from the Administrator of the 1st Southern General Hospital and from the headquarters of the Southern Command.

The third speaker was Mabel Verney. She started by saying how sorry she was when Lady Willoughby was obliged to retire owing to ill-health. She continued:

> Mrs Fielden (who continued as Commandant alone) had the courtesy and graciousness to consult Lady Willoughby on every point. They worked in perfect accord the whole of the time, but naturally the lion's share of the work fell to Mrs Fielden and she did not think any VAD hospital could have been worked more successfully than the one at Kineton. They all loved respected and looked up to her; and they had also to thank Mr Fielden, who not only gave his house and time, but something he liked

> better than anything, his wife. For four years he was shoved in the corner and put on one side, and had to find consolation by working in the kennels from morning to night. ... She now had the greatest pleasure in asking Mrs Fielden's acceptance of a convertible pendant-brooch (rubies and diamonds), together with a cheque, and a scroll (written by Mr Guernsey Webb) containing the names of 100 subscribers. Mrs Fielden received an ovation.[35]

Hospital honours at the Parish Church

A year after the end of the war, the flags which had hung so proudly over the hospital were placed in the church as a permanent memorial.

> The members of the Red Cross formed up outside the late Clarendon Hospital for church parade, headed by their Commandants, the Lady Willoughby de Broke OBE of the 8th division, and Mrs Fielden OBE of the 28th division, bearing the flags. Besides the members of the Red Cross, the ex-servicemen, the Comrades of the Great War, were especially invited to attend, and turned out in large numbers, also the boy scouts. Mr Webb presided at the organ, Colonel B Hanbury read the lessons, and the Vicar gave an excellent address.

At the end of the service

> the Vicar proceeded to the altar, followed by the commandants carrying the flags. These were handed to the Vicar, who placed them on the altar and blessed them. They are to be fixed on the capitals of pillars each side of the chancel arch.[36]

Whether they were placed in that position is not recorded, but until very recently one shabby flag which had once fluttered over Clarendon House VAD hospital hung above the brass War Memorial in St Peter's Church, Kineton.

It is clear that the Clarendon House VAD Hospital in Kineton was a fine example of what voluntary effort could achieve. That so many in the village of Kineton were able to sustain such a high level of commitment for four years is nothing less than remarkable. But the efforts at Clarendon House were being repeated in other small towns all over the country. Thousands of soldiers sent home to recuperate were thankful for the care of these small hospitals, and had they not been places of healing for mind and body, the outcome of the war might have been quite different.

ଔ

---

1 Report of the British Red Cross Society, 31 March 1916, pp. 12-25
2 *Parish Magazine of Burton Dassett et al (Parish Magazine)*, February 1910
3 ibid., November 1910
4 Janine Lawrence. Article in *www.hellfirecorner.co.uk*
5 *Stratford-upon-Avon Herald*, 31 December 1915, 26 May 1916, 4 August 1916 etc.
6 Report of the British Red Cross Society, 31 March 1916, pp. 12-25
7 ibid., p. 32
8 *Stratford-upon-Avon Herald*, 28 May 1915
9 *Warwickshire Advertiser*, 8 May 1915
10 *Parish Magazine*, February 1919
11 *Stratford-upon-Avon Herald*, 25 June 1915
12 ibid., 4 August 1916
13 ibid., 16 March 1917
14 *Warwickshire Advertiser*, 1 October 1915
15 Stevenson, John. *British Society* 1914-45 (Allen Lane : 1984) p. 79

[16] *Parish Magazine*, January 1916
[17] *Stratford-upon-Avon Herald*, 28 May 1915
[18] ibid., 1 June 1915
[19] ibid., 12 January 1917
[20] ibid., 17 August 1917
[21] ibid., 17 December 1915
[22] ibid., 25 October 1918
[23] ibid., 12 January 1917
[24] Janine Lawrence. Article in *www.hellfirecorner.co.uk*
[25] *Parish Magazine*, May 1915
[26] ibid., January 1917
[27] *Stratford-upon-Avon Herald*, 11 August 1916
[28] *Encyclopaedia Britannica*; also *Who's Who in the Theatre*, 1912-1976 (Pitman : 1978) p. 48
[29] *Stratford-upon-Avon Herald*, 17 August 1917
[30] ibid., 15 November 1918
[31] ibid., 22 November 1918
[32] ibid., 22 November 1918
[33] ibid., 21 February 1919 and 28 February 1919; also 5 September 1919
[34] ibid., 21 February 1919
[35] ibid., 28 February 1919
[36] ibid., 14 November 1919

1. *'C' Squadron of the Warwickshire Yeomanry leaving Coventry on 10th August en route for Warwick.*

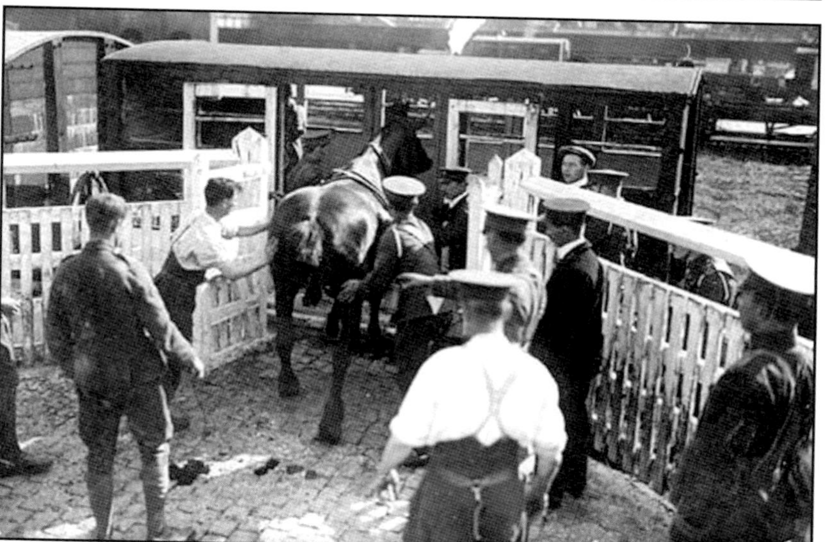

2. *Loading horses of the 5th Battery, 4th South Midland (Howitzer) Brigade, Royal Field Artillery, at Rugby Grand Central Station, 11th August, 1914. The initial destination of the Battery was Swindon.*

3. *Purchasing horses for the Army at Stourton. Undated but early in the war.*

4. *Whitley Abbey, Coventry, as it appeared at the start of the Great War.*

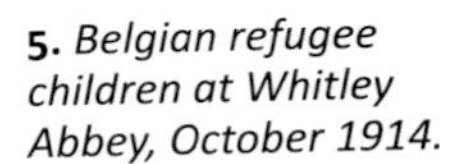

5. *Belgian refugee children at Whitley Abbey, October 1914.*

6. *A party of Belgian chaplains visiting Whitley in April 1915. Charles Mast, Superintendent of the home is at the centre of back row and his wife, Evelyn Mast, in front of him.*

7. *Arthur Sambrook, 1915.*

8. *Arthur Daulman, on leave from France, May 1916.*

9. *Members of the 216th Fortress Company photographed after a church parade; Nuneaton, 1915.*

10. *Members of the 216th Fortress Company drilling in Nuneaton.*

11. *Members of the 216th Fortress Company, 31st May, 1915. Captain F.C. Cooke seated in centre of group, with Company Sergeant-Major Mitchinson to his right and Corporal Wheway to his left.*

12. *Members of the 1st Battalion King's Own Scottish Borderers passing through Bilton during training. Undated – early 1915.*

13. *King George V with his entourage leaving Dunchurch station, on the morning of 12th March, 1915, on his way to inspect the 29th Division.*

14. *The wedding of Thomas Ash and Eleanor Garlick, Rugby, Christmas Day, 1917.*

15. *The grave of Private James Macdonald, King's Own Scottish Borderers, at Clifton Road Cemetery, Rugby.*

16. *The monument to the 29th Division, near Stretton on Dunsmore, which was unveiled on 24th March, 1921.*

17. *Walton Farm, Kineton, with Clarendon House to the right.*

18. *Hospital life at Kineton.*

19. *Kineton House: the building eventually held about 65 beds.*

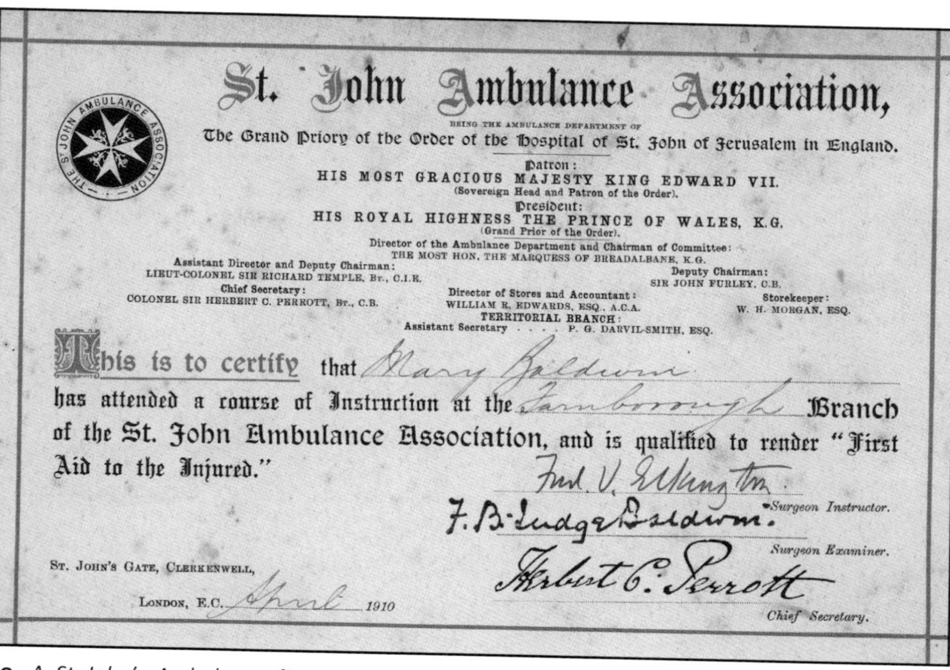

St. John Ambulance Association,

BEING THE AMBULANCE DEPARTMENT OF

The Grand Priory of the Order of the Hospital of St. John of Jerusalem in England.

Patron:
HIS MOST GRACIOUS MAJESTY KING EDWARD VII.
(Sovereign Head and Patron of the Order).

President:
HIS ROYAL HIGHNESS THE PRINCE OF WALES, K.G.
(Grand Prior of the Order).

Director of the Ambulance Department and Chairman of Committee:
THE MOST HON. THE MARQUESS OF BREADALBANE, K.G.

Assistant Director and Deputy Chairman:
LIEUT-COLONEL SIR RICHARD TEMPLE, BT., C.I.E.

Deputy Chairman:
SIR JOHN FURLEY, C.B.

Chief Secretary:
COLONEL SIR HERBERT C. PERROTT, BT., C.B.

Director of Stores and Accountant:
WILLIAM R. EDWARDS, ESQ., A.C.A.

Storekeeper:
W. H. MORGAN, ESQ.

TERRITORIAL BRANCH:
Assistant Secretary . . . . P. G. DARVIL-SMITH, ESQ.

This is to certify that Mary Baldwin has attended a course of Instruction at the Farnborough Branch of the St. John Ambulance Association, and is qualified to render "First Aid to the Injured."

Surgeon Instructor.

F. B. Judge Baldwin
Surgeon Examiner.

ST. JOHN'S GATE, CLERKENWELL,
LONDON, E.C. April 1910

Herbert C. Perrott
Chief Secretary.

20. *A St John's Ambulance first aid certificate from the first training course at Farnborough, Warwickshire.*

21. *The funeral cortège of Corporal Horace Thomas at Kineton, 19th November, 1918.*

THE WHITE & POPPE 4-CYLINDER 115 × 150 m/m SUBSIDY ENGINE.

Some thousands of these engines fitted in War Dept. lorries, have done wonderful service during the war with a phenominal record for economy and for the absence of necessity for overhaulage and repairs.

Two of these engines fitted in the Fire Pump House at our Holbrooks Lane Works constitute our protection against fire, each of them being capable of throwing 20,000 gallons of water per hour.

22. *The subsidy lorry engine being produced by White & Poppe Ltd from 1913. Built to War Office specification, its owners were eligible for a subsidy on the understanding that the vehicle was liable to be purchased by the War Office in time of war.*

23. *The Lockhurst Lane Factory of White & Poppe Ltd as it appeared in 1912.*

Chapter 6

Industry in Coventry

The wartime transformation of White & Poppe Ltd

Jeromy Hassell

ᏅᏫ

The founding of White & Poppe was initiated by Alfred James White, a son of Joseph White, the renowned Earlsdon watchmaker. Alfred first met Peter August Poppe in 1897 in Austria at the Steyr Works, a large manufacturer of small arms. Alfred, an engineer with the Swift Cycle Company Limited in Coventry, was there to negotiate a licence under which the Works would also manufacture Swift bicycles. Peter, a Norwegian engineer, was there on secondment from the Norwegian small arms factory in Konsberg. Both men were aged 27, and they quickly became friends. Alfred soon recognized Peter's true potential as an innovative engineer and suggested that the two of them should start an engine manufacturing business in Coventry.

White & Poppe Limited was established in late 1899 in Drake Street, off Lockhurst Lane (Figure 1). Before engine making could commence, the Boer War of 1899 to 1902 resulted in the new company securing large contracts to produce artillery fuse bodies, and the firm expanded rapidly. In its early days the firm pioneered the application of *the interchangeability of parts* to engine production. This required much greater accuracy in the casting and machining of parts, which had hitherto been filed and ground until they fitted. As a consequence the parts were then fully interchangeable between engines, and quicker assembly resulted.

During the years before the First World War, White & Poppe became the UK's largest makers of proprietory engines for the motor trade, supplying at least 48 manufacturers of road vehicles, as well as makers of aeroplanes, airships, locomotives and boats. Their most famous engine and power train was produced in 1913 for the first Morris car. This was the original *Morris Oxford*, nicknamed the Bullnose Morris. They also manufactured efficient carburettors, which sold in their thousands.

By the summer of 1914, White & Poppe were employing 350 people. Over the years, the Drake Street factory had been extended along Lockhurst Lane (Figure 2), and work had now started on building a new engine factory in green fields beside Holbrook Lane, Coventry.[1] The Company was then producing carburettors, the Morris power unit and nine

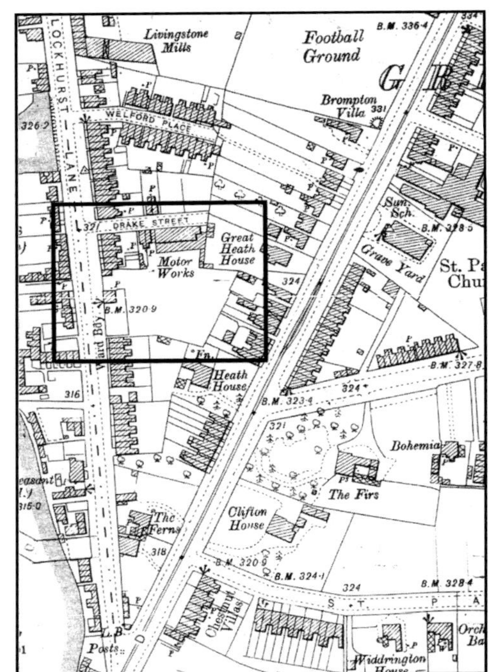

Figure 1: The Drake Street Factory: labelled as Motor Works (outlined in black). Ordnance Survey map of 1906. Crown Copyright Reserved.

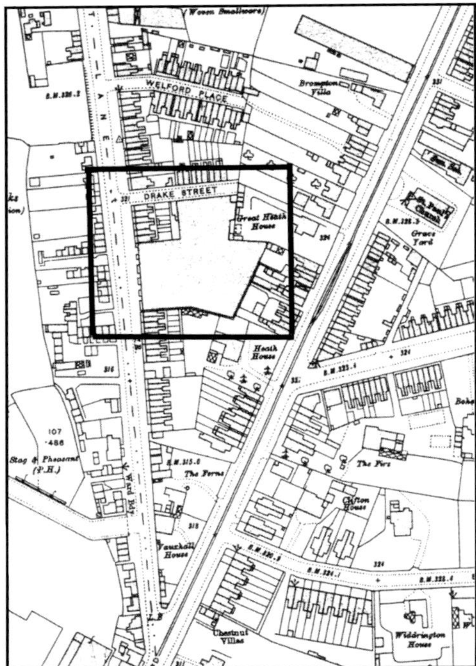

Figure 2: The Factory in 1913 (outlined in black), showing the extension along Lockhurst Lane. Ordnance Survey map of 1913. Crown Copyright Reserved.

other engine types, including a 4 cylinder 110mm bore by 150mm stroke *Subsidy Engine*, which had been launched in 1913. This engine was built to a War Office specification for use in lorries, whose owners were eligible for a subsidy on the understanding that the vehicle was liable to be purchased by the War Office in time of war. Three-ton trucks, which used this engine, were being built by Dennis Brothers. This was to be the first major war in which motor vehicles were to play a significant part.

When war was declared on 4 August 1914, Peter was away in Norway. Alfred cabled him and sent telegrams to all holidaying employees seeking their immediate return to work. He also instructed the drawing office to start preparing for the manufacture of bodies for Fuse 80. Although it was holiday time, the Subsidy Engine Department was back in full operation by 9 August. By the end of that month, the Company had a contract with Armstrong, Whitworth & Co to produce 10,000 aluminium Fuse 80 bodies and 10,000 brass 18 Pounder shell-sockets a week. About 12 draughtsmen worked in the Drawing Office at that time. Immediately, those who had been working on engines were switched to the preparation of drawings for fuse-bodies and shell-sockets, tools and jigs. Production of all but essential engines and carburettors was halted, and all available space was used for munitions machinery.

By October, demand for fuse-bodies had risen to 25,000 per week, and pressure for space had become critical, as orders for Subsidy engines had also now increased. Machines were packed together so closely that it was impossible to walk through the machine shops without being splashed with lubricant. By December, the demand for fuse-bodies had grown again to 43,000 per week, and the Transport and Progress Department was crammed with stacked fuse bodies, sockets and engine parts.

An extension of steel girders, clad with corrugated iron, was built on the flat roof of the Lockhurst Lane factory, while production continued unabated. The house next-door to it was demolished and stores built in its place. The firm also expanded into premises loaned by Courtaulds and other premises in Trafalgar Street. Alfred Herbert Limited helped in the manufacture of wooden trays for transporting bodies and sockets, and another building in Lower Ford Street was acquired for their production.

Problems were at first encountered during the machining of fuse bodies, because of the poor quality of the aluminium supplied. This contained hard pieces known as *diamonds*. These destroyed the lathes' cutting tools and caused sparks that often ignited the lubricating oil, resulting in the machine having to be dismantled and rebuilt. Eventually, *diamonds* were eliminated from the metal. Lack of brass throughout the Country, and its poor quality also hindered the manufacture of shell-sockets, but supplies and quality soon improved.

Demand had increased to such an extent that, at the end of 1914, it was agreed that a factory solely for the production of fuse bodies should be built along-side White & Poppe's new Holbrook Lane Engine Factory. This would release more space in the old Lockhurst Lane factory for Subsidy Engine production. This new factory, known as 8AM, was to mark the beginning of the first of three phases of developing a munitions works, which would eventually employ some 12,000 people.

The building of 8AM was to be financed by the Government through Armstrong Whitworth, and the property was to be leased to White & Poppe, with an option to purchase it at the end of hostilities.[2] For this and later phases of construction the architects were Harry Quick and Percival C Blow, who also designed the Singer factory, and the contractor was J G Gray. Work was started on 21 March 1915. This was a busy time, and a new order for 10,000 steel fuse-bodies per week was placed with them. This quickly grew to 30,000 per week.

As work progressed, cases containing new machinery were delivered and left unpacked in the adjacent field until they could be installed. By the end of June, the factory was in partial operation, with an initial workforce of about 30 girls. It was fully operational by August, and existing machinery was moved from Lockhurst Lane between shifts, without a drop in output. An order for 110,000 brass rings also arrived that month.

In the spring of 1915, White & Poppe had been asked to prepare for the manufacture of other fuse-bodies, and so work was started on building another factory (8XM). A third factory (8X3) was then built for the production of rings, caps and base-plugs, and in due course, the fourth, fifth and sixth factories were also built. They were designed as units measuring 420ft by 160ft, with north-facing lights in *saw-tooth* roofs. Figure 3 shows the whole of the finished site as it was after the War. The 6 factories can be seen running east-west on the map, beneath and to the north of the label *Dunlop Works* (a post-War occupant). To their north and south were the cottages and hostels housing the workforce.

Railway sidings were eventually to run alongside all the factories. Within each, wooden trolley lines ran the length of the building, between the rows of machines. Another six trolley-lines ran transversely within the factories, with small turntables at the junctions. Before the sidings themselves were laid, the transportation of supplies by road from Foleshill Station to the site presented a great challenge. The congestion, caused by transferring 225 tons of freight each day from railway wagons to lorries, resulted in the overcrowded local station having to reduce civil rail-traffic by over three-quarters, until the sidings were in operation. The first siding on the Holbrook Lane site was completed in November 1915. Then the first works locomotive, named *Ciceter*, arrived, and was followed by *Sirdar*. However, track-laying and transport on the site remained a great problem throughout the winter of 1915-16 and even caused a labour dispute.

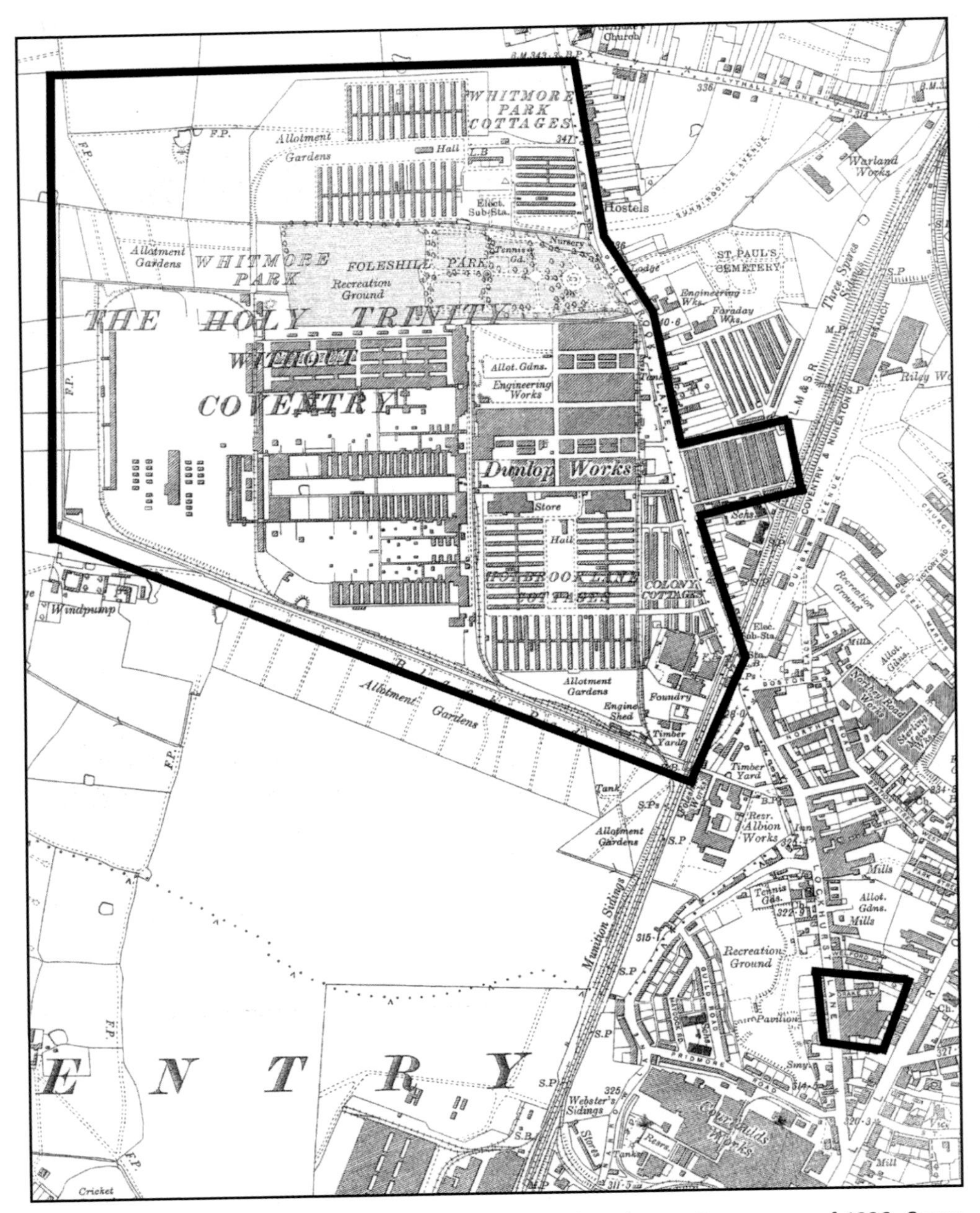

Figure 3: *The Holbrook Lane Factories (outlined in black). Ordnance Survey map of 1926. Crown Copyright Reserved.*

Because of the time-pressure, in places the track was levelled on almost anything, including pieces of brick and offcuts of wood. Soon, both locomotives were in urgent need of overhaul, and during the period 14-17 April 1916 over 200 wagons were being held at Foleshill Station, waiting to be hauled to the site. The problem was resolved by the arrival of a newer engine called *Bradford*.

Chapter 7

Food

Its production and control in the Kenilworth area, 1914-18

Susan Tall

Ꮳ

The First Months of War

At the outset of the First World War providing enough food for the British nation did not seem to be a problem. There was plenty of food in stock, certainly enough to last until Christmas, by which time some expected the war to be over. The harvest prospects in Kenilworth looked good. The wheat, barley and oats were said to be growing well, as were root vegetables, although the peas had been damaged by frost earlier in the year.[1] Difficulties would arise, however, if the length of the war was extended because of the quantity of food being imported from abroad. Britain had for many years imported more goods than she had exported and two-thirds of all Britain's food – most of the wheat, butter, meat, sugar, all the tea, and an increasing proportion of fruit and vegetables – had to be bought and shipped from abroad.[2]

One problem that did arise in the early days was people panic buying and hoarding food. An indignant letter to *The Times* complained of hundreds of shoppers at the Army & Navy stores on the day after war was declared laying in 'tons of provisions'.[3] These excessive purchases were not seen as justified by any actual or prospective shortage of foodstuffs. The withdrawal of continental supplies had raised the price of Danish bacon, eggs, butter and sugar, but there was sufficient wheat in the country to supply the whole population for four months and the cold stores were well filled with meat. The majority of the wheat supplies came from Canada, the US, the Argentine and Australia and the great bulk of fresh meat supplies from the Argentine and Australia. As long as Britain could maintain control of the Atlantic trade routes, the supplies of wheat and meat would scarcely diminish.[4]

Locally, in the first week of the war, the Mayor of Warwick was urging his townspeople not to give way to panic or to try to hoard up food supplies.[5] In Kenilworth, generally speaking, people were not rushing to the shops and had not taken in stores of provisions. The Co-operative Society was reported to have set an excellent example by maintaining the old prices, and discouraging large purchases.[6]

Within a few weeks, however, the British Government were beginning to think ahead to difficulties that might occur and started to encourage farmers, smallholders and allotment holders to grow more food at home, with the Board of Agriculture considering providing technical instruction for the inexperienced.[7] In October when farmers were preparing land for autumn and winter sowing, they were urged to increase their acreage of wheat. It was felt that, with less acreage being sown upon the continent, there would be an extra demand upon the world stock of wheat resulting in higher prices.[8]

The close of the year found people confident as regards the assured supply of their staple articles of food. Apprehension at the outset of war had been shown to be without foundation. If prices had gone up, they had not gone up to the extent that had been expected, and this rise was due to the cost of transport rather than the lack of supplies from abroad. Sugar from Germany was the only article of common consumption whose importation had been stopped and the Government had bought over 18 million pounds worth from other sources.[9]

The war, however, was not over by Christmas and in 1915 problems were beginning to arise. There was a shortage of ships to carry food from abroad as requisitioning for naval and military purposes took British shipping out of ordinary service. As a result, food prices started to go up.[10] The Germans also started their U-boat campaign in answer to the British blockade of their ports. They declared a war zone around the British Isles and started sinking any allied merchant vessel on sight. Fifty ships were sunk between February and September 1915, many of which were carrying food. It was only after the liner *Lusitania* was sunk, with the loss of 1,198 lives and the consequent American outrage, that the Germans – fearful of America joining the war – temporarily suspended their campaign.[11]

Schemes for increasing home food production

It now became more urgent to produce extra food at home, but many rural labourers had joined the forces at the beginning of the war and farms were left without enough manpower. This situation brought forward many ideas, schemes and plans for increasing home food production.

One suggestion was that women and children should be recruited for extra labour on the farms and the Board of Agriculture set up Women's War Agricultural Committees to organise recruitment. Women at that time were no longer working on general farms as they had done in the past and were chiefly working in market gardening and on fruit and vegetable farms. In some districts women still helped out with the hay and harvest in the summer but this was dying out with the use of machinery and even the milking and dairy work was now undertaken mostly by men. What farms really needed in the present war crisis was essentially considered man's work – ploughing and sowing, the handling of horses and machines and the care of animals. It was thought that the most effective help in the present crisis could be obtained from boys and it was suggested by the Chamber of Agriculture that children of 12 years and upwards might be exempted from school attendance during the continuance of the war, provided that they were employed solely on farms and returned to school at the earliest possible time.[12]

A further way to increase the food supply was made in an appeal to women living in villages and out of the way towns by the Joint Food Supply Committee of Associated Women's Societies. It was suggested that evening classes be started in the counties to teach the best methods of jam-making, pickling, preserving, poultry-rearing, bee keeping, fruit and vegetable growing, dairy work, etc. and also grading and packing for the market. Classes were already being formed and the Women's Agricultural Colleges agreed to supply teachers.[13] (This was in fact the beginnings of the Women's Institute, nowadays the largest national women's organisation in the UK.)

By May 1915, however, it was reported that the agricultural prospects in Warwickshire were 'not rosy'. The bad planting season the previous autumn and the shortage of labour had discouraged farmers from carrying out the Government's wishes to increase the area under wheat, and everywhere there were complaints of shortage of labour.[14] This scarcity led the Warwick Rural Council to agree to release roadmen for harvest work. Roadwork could not be carried out at that time because of a lack of material so it was possible to spare a large number of men. It was decided the surveyor should release as many men as possible for harvest and other agricultural work from the middle of June to the end of August.[15]

A scheme suggested by the Board of Agriculture was the formation of 'Village War Food Societies' which might be amalgamated, at least for the period of the war, with local gardening and allotment societies and might in some cases cover a group of villages. It was suggested that clerks to the parish councils call a meeting of interested residents with the purpose of forming a local society. The object of each society would be to ascertain the position of vacant building plots, uncultivated 'waste' areas and possibly even of common land, discover the owners and secure permission to cultivate the land. The society could arrange either for co-operative and mutual cultivation of the land and ownership of produce, or parcel it out to the members to cultivate for themselves individually. They could secure manure, seeds, plants, stocks, foodstuffs and implements on a co-operative basis and sell or preserve for home use the produce of their labours. Many suggestions were given by the Board of Agriculture such as breeding rabbits, keeping goats, pigs, poultry, or bees. Fruit could be preserved by either bottling, drying or converting it into jam with children being induced to take up the collection of wild fruits such as blackberries, wild raspberries, cranberries, whortleberries and crab apples. They could also collect acorns, horse chestnuts and beech nuts as useful foods for stock.[16]

The town of Kenilworth took up these suggestions and in October 1915 *The Kenilworth Advertiser* reported that the Noah's Ark Allotments, sited between School Lane and Albion Street, had successfully experimented with the purchase of seeds and manure in bulk and the President of the Association had suggested to his committee that they might enlarge upon this.[17]

The month of June 1915 saw a fall in wheat prices and bakers started to reduce the price of bread but, at the same time, the price of fresh meat rose because of the increased demands for meat by the British and French armies and of the shortage of vessels equipped for carrying meat from overseas. The Board of Trade called for people to eat less meat. In some places butchers were shutting their shops two days a week. In Coventry it was proposed butchers shut their shops on Mondays and Tuesdays.[18]

Harvest 1915

With summer and the harvest season approaching, various offers of help on farms were sent to the committee of Warwickshire Chamber of Agriculture and Stratford-upon-Avon District Farmers' Union, which had been formed to deal with the question of agricultural labour in Warwickshire. The London Teacher's Association offered people to help with haymaking, fruit picking and other lighter agricultural jobs in July and August. Likewise the headmaster of Rugby School, the Rev. Dr David, offered squads of five or six boys aged 16 to 18, working under a commander, to thin mangolds, to hoe, spud thistles and rake hay, within a reasonable distance of Rugby so that they could return to the school each evening. A Miss Creak from Bromsgrove was trying to organise women's war work in Birmingham and asked to be told of any Warwickshire farmers who would be glad of female labour for different kinds of farm work such as hay making, fruit picking or hop picking.[19]

The Army Council at this time ordered that furlough should be given, at the discretion of the military authorities, to a limited number of soldiers of the New Armies and of the territorial forces for work in the hay harvest as circumstances permitted. Farmers who wanted to employ soldiers could apply through their nearest Board of Trade.[20]

The Government also gave instructions to officers commanding districts that, to relieve the shortage of agricultural labour, certain men should not be induced to enlist. On farms where there was no one over recruitable age these would be a working farm bailiff or foreman, a head carter, horseman and second horseman in the case of a large farm, or waggoner, a head stockman or yardman, a shepherd and necessary millers (until either women or men not of recruitable age could be trained to take their places). Sufficient engine drivers, blacksmiths and thatchers should also be left as far as possible in every district. Postmen who wanted to work in the harvest could be granted a period of short leave for that purpose.[21]

In spite of these offers for help in Warwickshire, it was reported that the prospect of employing casual labour for the 1915 harvest was bad.[22] The weather conditions had not helped either. After a prolonged drought, heavy rain and wind had laid a great part of the crops. By September, however, the bulk of the wheat crop had been cut and was an average yield. Oats and barley were below normal, beans much blighted, peas moderate, potatoes an average yield. Turnips and swedes were below average. Mangolds however were above average as were apples, pears and plums. There had been wonderful crops of runner beans and the Royal Horticultural Society gave out advice on preserving them in salt in earthenware jars.[23]

The Coventry Grocer's Association in August 1915 reported that difficulties in the food markets appeared to be increasing. Bacon prices were up and, although there was a plentiful supply of imported ham and bacon from America, there was a considerable delay in shipping, together with a shortage of labour at the docks, so it was proving difficult to get really fresh supplies. Butter prices were also rising and lump sugar was practically unobtainable. The price of tinned tomatoes from Italy had risen, as Italy was now involved in the war and supplies were affected.[24] During August the cost of food had risen by 1% and the total cost of food since war started a year ago had risen by 35%, with marked increases in the price of bacon, butter, fish and eggs.[25]

Warwickshire County War Agricultural Committee

Towards the end of 1915 the Board of Agriculture and Fisheries, realising the war could well be prolonged, set up County War Agriculture Committees. The first meeting of the Warwickshire County War Agriculture Committee was held at Warwick on 13th November 1915 with Alderman Wheler-Galton as chairman. The scheme included appointing sub-committees in each borough and in each urban and rural district.[26]

Sir Sydney Olivier, Secretary of the Board of Agriculture and Fisheries, addressed this first meeting and said that fundamentally the purpose of the organisation was to try to maintain, and, if possible, increase the food production of the country, the importance of which was becoming greater and greater at the present time. The role of these County War Agricultural Committees and district committees was to facilitate farmers and agriculturists helping one another in their difficulties and to get assistance from the Board of Agriculture.

He thought the first matter the district committees had to deal with was to regularise and organise the labour supply. Since the introduction in October of Lord Derby's Recruitment Scheme to get more men to enlist, the Board of Agriculture and Fisheries had received a large number of enquiries from farmers as to its effect on agriculture. They had been reassured that certain classes of skilled agricultural workers had been starred in connection with the National Register and skilled and indispensable men would still be retained on farms. These starred men could get themselves put upon List B at their local recruiting office – that is on reserve. Such men would not be called upon until all other persons less indispensable had been called up.

This worsening situation led the Government to take active measures and they strengthened the Defence of the Realm Act (DORA) which had been passed at the beginning of the War and gave them emergency powers. The Board of Agriculture was now empowered to take and use vacant land for the purpose of food cultivation and local authorities were delegated to carry out this measure to increase the home-grown food supplies. Councils were given the right to take land and grow crops upon it as long as those crops only took up to a year to grow.[57]

Kenilworth War Allotments

As a consequence of DORA the town of Kenilworth started to take a far more active part in food production with Kenilworth Council passing a resolution that a War Allotments Committee be formed.

By January 1917 this was in full operation with members considering various sites around the town that could be used. There had been 126 applications for allotments from the townsfolk. Sites offered included a field in School Lane owned by Lord Clarendon, land in Whitemoor Road belonging to Mrs Whateley, a field in the centre of Abbey Fields, a small portion of land in Barrow Road belonging to Councillor Randall, land behind the Cherry Orchard brickyard belonging to Mr Hawke's executors and land in Bertie Road belonging to Sir Michael Lakin. Mr Cay had generously offered three acres of land at Windy Arbour rent free for the duration of the war. Twenty-four allotments were required in the St John's area of the town and Miss Schintz was approached about the land she owned there. She readily agreed to lend some of this and also offered to have it laid out into allotments.

Applicants would be allocated land as near their homes as possible and the suggested rent was 10s per fifth acre plot. The Allotments Committee proposed to purchase seed potatoes to sell at cost to the allotment holders. The Kenilworth Surveyor, Mr Sholto Douglas, was also given authority to grant permission to applicants to keep pigs provided they complied with the conditions recently published by the Board of Agriculture and the Local Government Board.[58]

Within a month of land being secured it had all been plotted out ready for digging once the frost had gone. Forty large plots and sixty-four small had been let and Mr Douglas had secured four tons each of King Edward (main crop) and Eclipse (early) seed potatoes, which would be sufficient to set about twelve acres of land.[59] On the 20th February, a very well-attended meeting was held at the Council Schools to hear a talk by Mr Dunkin, FRHS, the County Council expert, who gave a detailed and exhaustive lecture upon the best methods to produce the crops most needed: potatoes, peas, beans, carrots, parsnips, beet and different varieties of the cabbage family. He urged the gardeners to get the land broken up at once and recommended farmyard manure and soot and the need for frequent hoeing in summer time. He asked them all to work with a will, remembering the hardships of the long lines of heroes in France.[60]

Over the next few weeks most allotment holders put in strenuous work on their gardens with about half of them choosing to have their land ploughed. Councillor Randall had offered the use of one of his horses to assist in this ploughing when the weather permitted. Members of the Kenilworth Voluntary Training Corps were also called into action a week after Easter with the task of lending a helping hand to the wives of men on service who had no one to cultivate their gardens or allotments. *The Kenilworth Advertiser* described their activity as if the men were going into battle:

> 'Captain Chandler, Lieutenant Corser and Sergeant-major Beck, led fully forty members of the corps to the attack on Sunday afternoon, each shouldering a spade. Kenilworth people are familiar with the personnel of the local men, etc. nine out of ten quite unused to hard manual labour, and many of them getting on in life. It speaks volumes

for their training when the extent of ground dug in the 2½ hours of last Sunday afternoon is seen. They worked right heartily, and maintained the pace right through, digging over half-an-acre of land, and planting quite a deal of it too.'[61]

By the spring all the allotment holders had finished planting their crops and the potatoes were starting to come up.

Food Economy Campaigns

With the renewed U-boat campaign now preventing supplies reaching Britain, the food situation was becoming even more desperate. Enemy action sank 169 British and 204 Allied or neutral ships in April 1917. This represented 866,000 tons, or a quarter of all the tonnage using British ports. Enormous quantities of meat and grain en route to Britain had ended up on the ocean floor.[62]

At this point the country was only six weeks away from running out of wheat. The need to cut back on the amount of food eaten, particularly bread, was of great concern and the Government started a National Food Economy Campaign. Everyone was encouraged to reduce their consumption, with appeals for restraint and meatless days. Each citizen was implored to eat only 4 pounds of bread, two and a half pounds of meat and twelve ounces of sugar each week. A huge publicity campaign followed in newspapers, on billboard posters and in government propaganda films.[63]

Kenilworth set up its own Food Economy Campaign Committee in the spring of 1917 under the chairmanship of Dr Growse. A public meeting was held at the Abbey Hotel Hall in May when Mr E. J. Carter, H. M. Inspector of Schools, spoke of the necessity for cutting down on bread because of the difficulty of getting corn into the country and literature was distributed giving particulars of economical cookery.[64] A fortnight later a Food Economy Exhibition was held over three days in the Drill Hall when the ladies of Kenilworth were asked to supply cooked dishes with the recipes for making them.[65]

Even on Empire Day, the 24th May, the need for economy and frugality was stressed. A thousand Kenilworth schoolchildren assembled in the Abbey Fields where the chairman of the council, Mr Randall, read the King's Proclamation, exhorting and charging the people to practice the greatest economy and frugality in the use of every species of grain, to reduce the pre-war consumption of bread by at least a quarter, and to refrain from using flour for pastry, etc. In addressing the children Mr Randall asked them to eat as little bread as possible, and on no account to take any away from the table. All were asked, to sign a pledge to abide by the King's Proclamation, and to wear a purple ribbon as a sign of their patriotic intention. He further asked the children to refrain from buying sweets, for sugar was very scarce. 'Save your pennies', he said, 'and put them in the war savings, and so help your country.' By following on these lines he concluded they would be helping to defeat the enemy, whose object was to smash our Empire.[66]

Further Military Tribunals

Throughout 1917 the Military Tribunals were still being held on a regular basis. By now Kenilworth tradesmen as well as farmers were finding it increasingly difficult to run their businesses with so many of their employees having enlisted. Many appeared before the tribunal committee to appeal of behalf of their employees.

Mr Dowell, a local baker, applied for temporary exemption for John Twigger, aged 18, who had been passed for general service. Mr Dowell stated that he was already so short-handed in his bakery that should Twigger be called up he did not see how he could get through his work. He said that the young man was in the bakehouse from 5.15 a.m. to 12.30 p.m. and delivered bread in the afternoon. Mr George, a member of the tribunal, expressed the opinion that the system of delivery of bread was wasteful of labour. In

Coventry, he said, a system of pooling had been adopted, and only the biggest bakeries were now making bread. The application was refused.[67]

Likewise Mr Smith a farmer from Pleasuance Farm appeared before the tribunal to appeal for his wagoner, Norman Parkyn, aged 18. Mr Smith stated that he had 366 acres of land, 113 of which were arable land. He had planted 25 more acres of wheat than usual, and he urged the necessity of the lad remaining until the spring planting and summer cultivation had been finished. The military opposed on the ground that Mr Smith already had a lot of labour compared with other farmers, and that young healthy men were urgently required for the army. The application was refused, but the military undertook not to call him up until June 1st.[68] Norman's fate was sealed by this tribunal. He was called up later in 1917, went to France, and was taken a prisoner in March 1918, not being released until January 1919. His health by then had completely broken down and following a spell in hospital he died at home on 13th August 1920.

Kenilworth Allotments

By May 1917 most of the potatoes were well through and advice was given in *The Kenilworth Advertiser* that when the ground was dry to get the fork and hoe amongst the potatoes, to work in soot or sulphate of ammonia as soon as the rows could be discerned and gradually mould up the potatoes as they increased in height.[69] An appeal had also been made to potato growers by Mr Douglas, the Board of Agriculture's representative, to have their potatoes sprayed but the response had been very disappointing, even though he had met the members of each separate group of allotments and put the case for spraying before them. Careful trials had proved that potato spraying not only ensured sound crops, but actually gave increased returns far beyond the cost of the spraying. The Editor of the local newspaper in questioning the cause of this bad response commented that: 'Bluntly, it is sheer ignorance or carelessness; it is only too true that many people in the Midlands don't know there is a war on, or a submarine war.' The Noah's Ark Allotment Association, however, had responded favourably to the appeal and its members had decided unanimously that every garden should be sprayed. Townsfolk were keen to preserve fruit, however, and the Council had recently ordered another 200 dozen 2lb fruit-preserving bottles.[70]

Labour force for the 1917 harvest and the new Women's Land Army

In June 1917, the Food Production Department announced arrangements being made nationally for the supply of additional farm labour for the hay and corn harvests. The Army authorities had agreed to provide a number of soldiers, and civilians were being enrolled by the National Service Department. These civilians consisted of women, German prisoners of war, German civilian prisoners and conscientious objectors. There was also temporary assistance to be given by schoolchildren. It was felt that with all these various sources of supply no farmer should go short of labour.[71]

Women's involvement, which was still the largest potential source of labour in farm work, was greatly expanded during 1917. A new mobile uniformed Land Army was formed, consisting of women who were prepared to give their whole time and to go anywhere or undertake any agricultural work at the direction of the Board of Agriculture. The first appeal to women to join the Land Army was issued in March 1917 by the National Service Department and 40,000 women responded to the appeal (of whom only 5,000 were chosen, although numbers later increased to 23,000).[72] During the first few months the women met with considerable discouragement, through the prejudice of farmers and the uncertain demand for their labour. The demand, however, increased after the summer of 1917.[73]

In the early years of the war when women had first offered their services for work on the land they were asked to undertake 'light farm work' but as time went on, they more and more undertook the heaviest forms of labour. There was, moreover, a steady increase in their efficiency and on October 4th, 1917 a competition was held at Edgbaston, Warwickshire, for women land workers of the Midland counties to test their new learnt skills. There were several tests including a general labourer's test, a wagoner's test (including ploughing), a cow-woman's test (including milking by hand or machinery), and a machinery test (comprising tractor ploughing). The standard of the tests was approved by the Board of Agriculture, the National Farmers' Union and the Royal Agricultural Society, so that the certificates would be acceptable to farmers throughout the country. About 250 women farm workers entered for the tests and although 75% was necessary to secure an efficiency certificate and 70% for a highly commended certificate, in the milking tests not a single candidate failed. The results in regard to forms of labour usually regarded as less suited to women, such as ploughing, ridging, drilling and tractor driving, were almost equally striking. The proportion of women who failed in the tests was very small.[74]

In Kenilworth by the beginning of September 1917, 50% of the corn had been harvested although, as in previous years, it had been affected by the weather and most was laid flat. The potatoes were doing well and were not diseased. The approach of autumn had also resulted in a very heavy crop of blackberries and ever-mindful of the need to provide food, the Board of Education and the Food Production Department came up with a scheme for organising the collection of blackberries by schoolchildren to be made into jam for the troops. Half-holidays were granted to the children to go blackberry picking and it was hoped to carry on the scheme on each Friday during the month of September. The children brought the berries to stores which were established at the schools. They were weighed and paid for at the rate of 1d per pound.[75] After two weeks the schoolchildren of Kenilworth and the neighbouring villages had picked and sent off a magnificent 2,173 lbs of blackberries, and further half days of picking were planned.[76]

Kenilworth Food Control Committee

By the end of 1917, the supply of food was still an increasing problem throughout the country. The Food Controller launched a further economy campaign, although the Kenilworth Food Control Committee were of the opinion that he should have adopted immediate rationing in view of the apparent failure of the last economy campaign. They elected an economy sub-committee and fixed the prices of butter and potatoes as well as the maximum meat prices for the district.[77]

They urged the townsfolk to exercise economy in everything. It was becoming difficult to obtain a sufficient supply of milk, as pasture land was now coming under the plough and there were instances of families in which there were young children going short, while other families consisting of adults were getting all the milk they required.[78] The Food Control Committee now formulated a tentative scheme under which milk supplies would be ensured for infants, invalids and nursing mothers.[79]

Flour for bread making was also difficult to obtain and bakers were having to resort to adding a quantity of potatoes to the bread mix. The committee stressed that generally speaking it was found that bread so constituted had an improved flavour, unless the percentage of potato flour was excessive.[80]

Just before Christmas 1917, Kenilworth Council held a special meeting to consider opening a communal kitchen in the town. An experimental National Kitchen had already been set up in London earlier in the year, which was designed to make sure working mothers and their children were fed properly.[81] A Kenilworth Communal Kitchen was seen as a further aim at economy by cooking in bulk and aimed to help those people who with longer working hours were hard pressed to find time for cooking. The kitchen would be self-supporting, with those benefitting paying the cost of their meals. The Food Control Committee asked the Council for two ground-floor rooms and the loft over them in the cottage adjoining the council office. They asked for this to be provided rent-free with the

ensure that the business and work of officials and claimants would be unaffected. In the tribunal's early days sittings took place on Thursdays, changed to Wednesdays when it was discovered that Thursday sittings clashed with those of the County Appeals Tribunal. As some of the Borough Tribunal members were also magistrates, Wednesdays would be very trying indeed, since that was court day too.

The tribunal of 30 March 1916 was attended by an insufficient number of members. Only three members sat, attended by Robert Lunn and Mr Talbot for the military. Winter suggested that the Borough Council should appoint two further members. Savage suggested a Labour man, but Winter referred the decision to the Borough Council.[14] Accordingly, at its meeting on 11 April 1916, the Council made the following appointments: Councillor G.W. Everard, Mr F. Cranmer and Mr W. Hughes (replacing Metters who could not attend on a regular basis).[15] Later in the year, Alderman Flower suggested the appointment of Councillor Edward Fox to the tribunal, which was carried.[16] Thus the Stratford-upon-Avon Borough Local Tribunal was established.

The members of the tribunal had a difficult task to perform and few could have envied them their task. Their decisions would not necessarily send men to the front line: the Army would decide that. What they *were* deciding, using their own judgment and evidence presented to them, was whether a man should serve at all. A poor decision could result in financial or business ruin for a claimant or severe hardship for his dependents. Their role was therefore often thankless and undoubtedly they made many enemies while dispensing justice among their neighbours and fellow townspeople, some of whom they would have known well. Nevertheless, however difficult their decisions, it was their responsibility to carry out the government policy of filling the Army's ranks so that the war could be brought to a speedy end. They would also be required to balance the needs of the town of Stratford-upon-Avon against the military's demands.

Judging by reports in the *Stratford-upon-Avon Herald*, the tribunal performed its duties impartially and 'without fear or favour', and on occasions when a member had an interest, then his withdrawal from the hearing was conscientiously adhered to. Alderman Flower, the owner of Flower's Brewery, was the employer of many of the claimants appearing before the tribunal and always withdrew in such cases. When the Corporation applied for exemption for their only remaining carpenter (forty-six year old Thomas Stanley) in 1918, Flower referred the case to the Stratford Rural District Tribunal as three of the four Borough Tribunal members were also members of the Corporation.

Tribunal hearings were held in public except, rare in Stratford's case, when the claimant asked for a private hearing. There are no reports to show that the viewing public was anything other than well behaved at the Borough Tribunal. On the other hand, at the first sitting of the Stratford Rural District Tribunal at the Boardroom of Arden House (the old workhouse), the Chairman, Mr Couchman, declared that he '... deprecated the practice of canvassing Tribunal members prior to hearings. A practice that is not proper and [is] useless.'[17]

Although the tribunal members dispensed with cases as equitably as they could, things did not always run smoothly. Over a six-month period, from November 1916 to May 1917, a number of altercations arose, all initiated by Cranmer, concerning claims of unfairness and double standards on the part of the tribunal and the military representatives. Later he complained about procedural irregularities and matters came to a head on 9 May when he again criticised the tribunal for applying double standards in its decision making. Despite two separate public statements by the tribunal chairmen that each case was dealt with on its merits, Cranmer remained unconvinced: he left the meeting of 9 May, and did not sit on the tribunal again.[18]

If Cranmer's behaviour had proved an annoyance to the tribunal, then the announcement at the sitting of 20 September 1916 that its clerk, Robert Lunn, had received his call-up papers, must have come as something of an embarrassment. Nevertheless, the military representative assented to Lunn's claim for exemption and the clerk received a conditional exemption. The condition was (presumably) that he was to continue to perform his duties as clerk to the tribunal.[19]

One of the responsibilities of the military representatives was to provide substitute workers for employers whose work-force had been seriously reduced. Some employers were not satisfied with these replacements and a committee of tribunal members was set up on 24 November 1916 to provide mediation. This committee comprised all tribunal members except Messrs Flower and Winter.[20]

By the second half of 1917 the sittings of the tribunal were becoming less regular. Some heard no claims at all, only applications from the military representatives for reviews of cases, and requests for amendments to temporary exemptions. This was not because there was less demand for men to serve but that most of those eligible for conscription had already received their call-up and were either serving or had had their claims processed. Sittings therefore became fewer as time went on and on 9 October 1918 Lunn read to the tribunal a letter from the Local Government Board advocating the principle of amalgamation. The Board suggested a merger of tribunals across south-east Warwickshire to comprise six members from Stratford Borough, two from Brailes, two from Stratford Rural District and one from Farnborough. This was accepted but no such amalgamation took place as the war came to an end one month later.

In total, 809 claims were reported in the *Stratford-upon-Avon Herald*. Also reported were reviews and requests to appeal but these have not been included in the following analysis. Non-contentious claims, dealt with by the clerk or military representative, were not reported by the newspaper and are therefore also excluded.

The workload of tribunals varied. It is known, for instance, that the Leeds tribunal dealt with an average of 120 cases daily (with about 50 per cent resulting in refusals).[21] In comparison the Borough tribunal, with an average of twenty-five cases per weekly sitting, was very quiet though this is hardly surprising given the difference in populations. Claimants came from a wide range of occupations, including waggoners, wheelwrights, colporteurs, brewery workers, brewers' chemists, steam plough drivers, coopers and gas works employees. A large proportion of claimants, some 12.3 per cent, was engaged in agricultural work and 26.6 per cent worked in the retail or retail supply sector. Skilled and unskilled men represented 23.2 per cent and 20 per cent respectively. Although there was a reduction in available manpower during the war, it would appear that trade in Stratford-upon-Avon did not suffer too greatly. Ages of claimants ranged from eighteen to fifty-one, with an annual average of 33.1 in 1916, 32.8 in 1917 and 41.9 in 1918 (following the increase in the upper age limits for conscripts to fifty).

Employers lodging a claim accounted for 43.5 per cent of cases, with individuals' claims making up the remainder. Claims for being in a reserved occupation were few, with just 3.6 per cent of claims on that ground. Domestic and financial reasons for a claim made up 11.4 per cent. The large number of claims for unfitness or invalidity, 16.2 per cent, represents both the general poor state of health of the nation at that time and the demand for older men in the war's later stages. Conscientious objection amounted to just 0.8 per cent of claims, all of which were on religious, rather than political or ethical grounds. The bulk of the claims, 63.6 per cent, were to do with business, either that trade would suffer or that an employee was indispensable.

With so little documentation surviving from tribunals, it is difficult to determine whether or not the Borough tribunal was typical in the way it disposed of claims. Only 4.2 per cent of claimants received absolute exemption and 12.2. per cent of claims were refused. Claimants granted conditional exemptions made up 23 per cent of the total and temporary exemptions 43 per cent. All remaining claims were either adjourned or withdrawn. When it is considered that two thirds of claimants received a conditional or temporary exemption, it would appear that the tribunal acted fairly, if not leniently.

The *Stratford-upon-Avon Herald* reported no obviously frivolous claims made to the tribunal. As might be expected, the majority of claims were made soon after conscription was introduced and men began receiving call-up papers. At the very first tribunal hearing C.H. Bullard, a Quaker living in Henley Street, claimed absolute exemption on the grounds of conscientious objection. He was granted a non-combatant exemption.[22] His appeal to the County Appeals Tribunal was unsuccessful. His son recalled that '... the tribunals ... didn't give much in the way of exemption'.[23] Forced into the Army, albeit as a non-combatant, Bullard refused to conform and was court-martialled and imprisoned.[24] Another conscientious objector did receive an absolute exemption: J. Ready, aged forty, an itinerant evangelist and colporteur.[25]

The case of A.L. Pearce demonstrates the administrative efficiency of the appeals process. His written claim for absolute exemption was entered on 21 February 1916. The military representative, Major Bairnsfather, disagreed, so the claim was processed on 26 February and heard on 2 March. Pearce received a three-month temporary exemption for him to put his business in order. On 9 March the military representative, this time Mr Talbot, appealed against Pearce's temporary exemption. The appeal was heard on 23 March and the original exemption allowed to stand.[26] In less than one month the whole claim and appeal process had been completed.

When, in January 1917, the employers of twenty-eight-year-old shoesmith, William Melburne, asked for an extension to a temporary exemption he had received, they claimed he was indispensable to their business of supplying six hundredweight of agricultural and military horseshoes per month, work considered to be of national importance. Captain Bros, the military representative, suggested that Melburne might be employed as a smith by the Army. A conditional exemption was granted, but only on condition that the company, Messrs Hutchings and Co., produce six hundredweight of shoes up to the end of February and nine hundredweight monthly thereafter.[27]

Evidence that the government was seeking to call-up as many men as possible is found in the case of two applicants who had previously volunteered for the Army (one of them twice) but who had initially been rejected on medical grounds due to their stature. John Bone, aged twenty-seven, and Charles Guise were 4 ft 11 ins and 4 ft 9 ins tall respectively. Bone weighed just 94 pounds (an infantryman's fighting equipment weighed 66 pounds). On their call-up in 1916, both now claimed unfitness as grounds for exemption. Whether this was because their initial enthusiasm had waned (by that time the war had entered its third year with no end in sight) or because they resented such a demand after their earlier rejection may never be known: both, though, received exemptions.[28]

Arthur Fletcher, a twenty-one-year-old painter and decorator had only one eye, but had been passed fit for military service. Although his claim on grounds of unfitness had been supported by Mr Savage, the tribunal decided that Fletcher should serve when it was brought to its attention that the military representative of the day, Mr Talbot, was blind in one eye but had served with the local volunteers.[29] Military representatives were eager to get as many men as possible into the Army's ranks and would go to some lengths to ensure that claims for unfitness were authentic. James Henry Brooks, for example, a thirty-six-year-old foreman cooper with a severe rupture, was sent to successive medical examinations locally and as far away as London.[30]

A good amount of banter and badinage was exchanged during the hearings, some serious and cutting, some not. Mr Williams, the employer of forty-five-year-old Charles Marshall, a tailor, had suffered staff shortages due to the war and he claimed Marshall as indispensable. Mr Jackson, the military representative, commented that if the Germans got to England Williams would not require Marshall nor anyone else. Part of Marshall's work was to make trousers and breeches for Army officers and Williams declared: 'Officers can't fight without clothes!' 'Can't they?' retorted Jackson. Marshall gained a three-month exemption.[31]

An example of a rather perplexing claim was made by F.A. Southam. He was a thirty-year-old widower employed as a labourer at Flower's Brewery. He had been passed fit for military service but claimed exemption on domestic grounds as he had two young children to care for. His case was adjourned for two weeks so that he could make arrangements for his children's welfare. When the case re-opened on 28 March 1917 the fact came to light that Southam's younger child had died two months previously and Southam could give no explanation why he had not informed the tribunal of this at the earlier hearing. His claim was refused.[32]

As a final case study, the brothers Frank and William Eborall of the Oddfellows Arms in Windsor Street appeared together at the tribunal on 17 May 1916. Frank wished to withdraw his claim for exemption and was willing to serve on condition that his brother be exempted. William, however, thought that, as he was single, he should go and his brother should stay to run the public house and the small on-site brewery. Mr Everard acknowledged that it was '... refreshing to find two young men willing to serve...' and asked: 'Can't they both go?' It was decided that William would serve and that Frank would receive a conditional exemption so long as his brother remained in the Army.[33]

The last sitting of the Stratford-upon-Avon Borough Tribunal took place on 23 October 1918 and no reference to it subsequently appeared in the *Stratford-upon-Avon Herald*. Nor have any personal papers been identified that allude to the tribunal. Its members had performed their onerous duties conscientiously and, given the high proportion of various exemptions, with genuine humanity. It has not proved possible to follow through what happened to those who received temporary exemptions: some certainly went on to serve in the Army. Nevertheless, as well as providing men for the military, the tribunal had shown awareness for the interests of Stratford-upon-Avon and its people.[13]

~

This article was first published in Warwickshire History (The Journal of the Warwickshire Local History Society), Volume IX, Number IV, Winter 2000-2001 and is reprinted here with the Society's kind permission.

ᏣᏰ

---

1 Winter, quoting his source as PRO, Ministry of National Service Papers, NATS 1/400, calculates that, after adjustments for those unavailable for military service, only 24.59 per cent attested under the Derby Scheme: J.M. Winter, *The Great War and the British People*, London 1985.

2 *Stratford-upon-Avon Herald*, 28 January 1916. The time limits were strictly adhered to during all stages of a claim or appeal. Any claims 'out of time' were not proceeded with and military service ensued.

3 *Stratford-upon-Avon Herald*, 14 January 1916, reporting a meeting of 12 January between Prime Minister Asquith and others where details of the Military Service Bill were discussed.

4 A claimant in Leeds claimed exemption because he had started a course of hair tonic which required three months for results to show and that he had certain domestic commitments; for example, he had to give his wife tea in bed: D. Winter, *Deaths Men: Soldiers of the Great War*, London 1979, p.30. Not all claims were for exemption; also in Leeds wives were writing to tribunals asking that their husbands be sent to serve! E.S. Turner, *Dear Old Blighty*, London 1980, p.174.

5 Local Tribunals were set up across south Warwickshire for Alcester, Kenilworth, Warwick, Leamington Spa, Warwick Rural District, Brailes Rural District, Farnborough Rural District and Marston Sicca District.

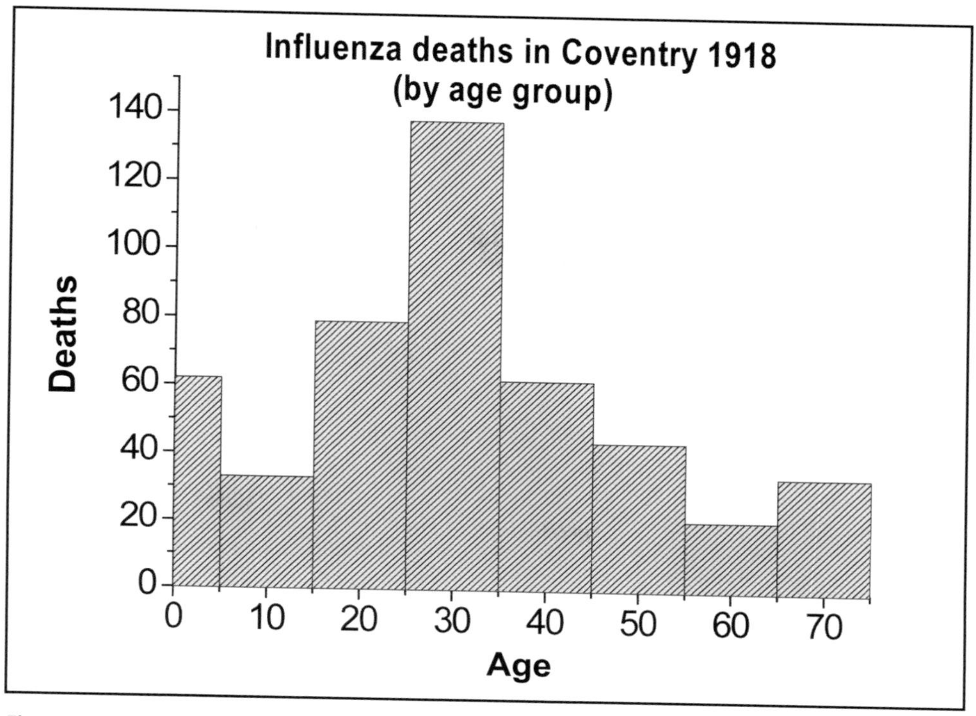

Figure 2: *Influenza deaths in Coventry, 1918, by age group. (Based on E.H. Snell:* City of Coventry: Annual Report on the Health of the City, 1918.*)*

The Board's Chief Medical Officer, Sir Arthur Newsholme, speaking to the Royal Society of Medicine on 13 November, argued that the "relentless needs of warfare" and the "need to carry on" justified the risk of spreading infection. He was not alone in that view: "the maintenance of normal social and economic life was integral to medical orthodoxy regarding influenza in 1918-19".[22]

Locally, the main action that the authorities took was simply to pass on the official advice from the Local Government Board on how to avoid influenza or how to deal with it once the disease had been caught (see Illustration 26). Local variations existed on these common themes. In Nuneaton, point 6 on the list of suggestions on "How To Avoid Influenza", in which people were urged "Do not be afraid of influenza", was replaced by the invocation: "Avoid intoxicating liquors and eat plenty of nourishing food. Porridge is desirable."[23] By comparison, the Rugby Housewives' Committee was assured by "a medical practitioner" that: "It has been noticed that large eaters of onions do not take any infection of any kind".[24]

How much value these lists had was sometimes questioned by medical authorities themselves. Commenting on the Local Government Board's guidelines, Dr E.H. Snell, Coventry's Medical Officer of Health, concluded that: "So little is known concerning how the illness can be averted that it is doubtful to what extent these could have any influence on the spread of the epidemic".[25] The *Rugby Advertiser* of 2 November reported Dr Darley, Acting Medical Officer for Crick Rural District Council, as saying that local inhabitants never read the circular but used it instead to light their fires!

In the absence of any real understanding of what caused the disease, there was no shortage of more general suggestions as to what was contributing to its deleterious impact. On 25 October, the *Stratford-upon-Avon Herald* suggested that the onset of winter, coupled with shortages of food, fuel and warm clothing, made people "less able to resist attacks from the microbe". In a letter to the *Nuneaton Observer* of 8 November, Mr W.F. Knight of Manor Court Baptist Church argued that "The epidemic has been a sad revelation of the horrible conditions under which dozens of Nuneaton families live", before asking what action the Town Council was planning to take on the matter. Similarly, the *Nuneaton Observer* for 22 November quoted a local doctor who felt that overcrowding and the filthy conditions in which many people had to live lowered their resistance, along with the strain of war. Editorial comment in the *Nuneaton Observer* on 21 February, 1919, gave the outbreak an additional political dimension: "When we get the Ministry of Health set up, we may expect drastic steps to prevent these constant outbreaks."

Although living conditions were often appalling, the *Rugby Advertiser* for 2 November noted that victims were largely to be found "among people whose means, one would surmise, would enable them to live as well as rationing regulations will permit and engaged in healthy occupations". In his report for 1918, Dr E.H. Snell noted dispassionately that influenza cases were distributed throughout the city, irrespective it would seem, of prevailing living standards.[26] In this respect, his observations were in keeping with conclusions subsequently reached at a national level. The 1920 report by the Registrar-General for England and Wales noted that "the mortality of the late epidemic fell almost alike on the sanitary just and unjust".[27] The virus was so virulent that overcrowding was not necessarily an issue, although enclosed communities, such as internment camps and workhouses, could experience high rates of infection. In November 1918, during the worst of the outbreak, Coventry's Medical Officer of Health had also reported that he could find no link between fatalities and occupations.[28]

The influenza virus was not isolated until 1933; in consequence, contemporaries had little understanding of the real causes of the disease. References are to "germs" and "microbes", which were associated especially with the upper respiratory tracts, hence the common recommendations about gargling and nasal douching.

Although influenza was recognised as a "crowd disease", very few practical steps were taken at a local level to try to reduce the spread of infection. Once the disease had become established in the country, it seems unlikely that local measures would have had much chance of success.[29] At the meeting of the Coventry Watch Committee on 6 November, 1918, it was resolved to ensure that Coventry's cinemas should refuse admission to children under the age of 14. This restriction remained in force until 15 January, 1919. Further, the city's Sanitary Committee was requested to instruct their officers to inspect and report upon the efficiency of ventilation in cinemas.[30] At a meeting of the Nuneaton Town Council on 6 November, Dr A.A. Wood, the town's Acting Medical Officer of Health, also said that he would like to see children under the age of 14 excluded from cinemas; however, no action was taken, as the Town Clerk was of the opinion that the Council had no power to make such an order.[31] Local Government Board regulations introduced later in November did permit the regulation of cinemas but no action appears to have been taken in Nuneaton.

Apart from general advice to avoid unventilated assembly rooms and places of entertainment, it does not appear that local authorities placed – or even considered – specific restrictions on other crowded venues and it has been argued that measures directed against cinemas "reflected anti-vice concerns regarding the perceived immorality of cinemas rather than sound public health".[32] One proprietor in Coventry protested to the Watch Committee against the exclusion of children under 14, whilst Mr A. Spencer unsuccessfully petitioned the Committee to lift the ban in the case of the Opera House, which had been preparing for the Children's Christmas Pantomime.[33] In general, cinemas sought to assure their customers that they were clean and well-ventilated, whilst readers of the *Coventry Herald* were told that: "At many places of entertainment the audiences are frequently sprayed with disinfectant".[34] On 2 November, the *Rugby Advertiser* reported that, notwithstanding the prevalence of the 'flu, the town's Palace Cinema "was still going strong". Considering the severity of the outbreak, cinemas and other places of entertainment seem to have continued much as usual.

If very little was done to try to prevent the spread of the disease, then even less was done by the local authorities to mitigate its effects. The Coventry and Warwickshire Hospital did place some of their wards at the disposal of patients suffering from pneumonia, although it was admitted by the Medical Officer of Health for Coventry that the type of pneumonia prevalent was so severe that hospital provision appeared to have little influence in checking a fatal ending. Indeed, some argued that removal of pneumonia patients to hospital was itself harmful.[35] In Rugby, a temporary hospital for influenza cases was opened by the Health Committee of the Rugby Urban District Council. On 4 November, the Mitchinson Homes, in Cromwell Road, Rugby, were put under the charge of Mrs H.C. Bradby, who was assisted by two paid nurses. By 9 November, six patients had been admitted. Another house, in Hillmorton Road, was being held in readiness for emergencies. Concerns were expressed by a number of local residents and the Health Committee sought to reassure these people that the temporary hospital posed no threat to their well being.[36] However, it would appear that this provision of additional accommodation for some of the most serious cases in Coventry and Rugby was unusual and no similar facilities have been noted as being provided by other authorities in the area.

Assistance of a different kind was provided in Rugby in early November, when six additional men had been taken on to assist the two grave diggers normally employed at Rugby Cemetery.[37] The *Coventry Standard* for 30/31 November reported that half a dozen soldiers from Budbrooke Barracks had been assisting in grave digging, replacing the first batch of about a dozen soldiers. A number of temporary labourers had also been engaged. The newspaper emphasised that the all burials took place in daylight and that reports to the contrary were exaggerated.

Sandra Tomkins has argued that the official British response to the pandemic was "lacklustre", with too much emphasis being placed on trying to prevent the spread of influenza and too little on alleviating distress. She cites the examples of a number of councils in London, such as Bethnal Green and Fulham, where more active policies were pursued, including the provision of home nursing services.[38] However, a glimpse of some of the practical problems facing the authorities can be seen in the report on a meeting of the Coventry Council on 26 November. Only 18 members of the Council were present, out of a full muster of 48, although not all absentees were influenza victims. During the meeting, Mr Hook asked if nurses could not be employed to attend cases where influenza victims had no-one to look after them. In response, Mr Makepeace said that if Mr Hook could let the Sanitary Committee know where two or three hundred nurses could be obtained, then he would be very grateful, adding that: "Nurses could not be got for love nor money".[39] In Rugby, the Urban District Council appealed in late October for volunteers to help visit the sick and offset the shortage of nurses.[40] A week later, the same Council was considering writing to the Local Government Board on the need for more nurses; an additional dozen or twenty would be a "Godsend". Another of the Council's concerns was who would pay for any additional expenditure.[41] In general, one senses that the speed, severity and scale of the outbreaks, especially the one in the autumn, simply overwhelmed the authorities, with politicians usually content to be advised by the Medical Officers of Health, in turn largely dependent upon official advice from the Local Government Board. In this respect, it would appear that Coventry and Warwickshire were probably little different to most parts of the country.

In dealing with the disease, medical authorities had little to offer beyond sympathy and common sense advice, such as victims taking to their beds and remaining there until a full recovery had been made. In the absence of effective medicines, there was no shortage of commercial 'solutions', as advertisements in local newspapers show. In order "To Prevent Influenza" one could order a good overcoat from G.C. Dean, a tailor in Cross Cheaping in Coventry. "Disease germs" would find no "lurking place" when Lifebuoy Soap had been used, while those "deprived of the body building powers of Bovril" might easily fall victim to the epidemic. Regrettably, a shortage of bottles had reduced the availability of the beverage and was thus hampering Bovril Ltd's efforts to combat the epidemic. Fortunately, those deprived of their Bovril could turn to Chymol, a "pure, delicious super-food", which not only built up natural resistance to influenza but guarded against its after-effects. If the combination of Chymol's "red bone marrow, sweet fats and fine barley malt" proved unpalatable, then Professor B.M. Smith, "The Great African Medical Herbalist", could offer a cure to Spanish Influenza. Retailing at 3s 9d, even the first bottle of his panacea would cure – as long as it was taken "before the disease develops"!

The economic and social impact

Very high sickness rates would have had a significant, short-term impact on the local economy and social life. However, specific details are hard to come by, most references to the disruption of local industries, mines and the like being of a general nature. Whilst the country was still at war, this is probably understandable. However, the *Rugby Advertiser* for 2 November did report that 900 employees at B.T.H. and 200 at Willans and Robinson's were suffering from the influenza. The *Nuneaton Observer* for 22 November noted, with a certain pride, that the edition had been produced by two men on the mechanical side and one on the literary side, the rest being victims of the 'flu. Assuming that about half the population were taken ill with influenza, it seems likely that, at some point, half the work force were forced to take time off. In Rugby, a shortage of volunteers delayed the issue of new ration books.[42] Amongst the inconveniences noted by the *Stratford-upon-Avon Herald* were the fact that "workmen for a time were unobtainable" and that "many houses had their domestics incapacitated".[43]

Inevitably, the disease affected education. School attendances were greatly reduced as children fell sick, although the Medical Officer for Health for Coventry noted that a large number of children were kept at home to lend help to stricken households.[44] As stated, nearly half Bedworth's school children were absent in July 1918 and all Nuneaton's schools were closed in November on the recommendation of the town's Medical Officer of Health.[45] In Warwick Urban District, 6 elementary schools were closed in the summer outbreak and all of them in the outbreak later that same year.[46] In Southam Rural District, 5 schools were closed in the summer, 11 at some point in the last three months of the year.[47] (However, the annual reports by local Medical Officers of Health show that during 1918 school closures were also being caused by a variety of other illnesses, notably whooping cough, measles, scarlet fever, chicken pox and mumps.) As late as March 1919, Stockingford schools were badly affected by the outbreak of influenza among teachers.[48]

Long Itchington lost two of its teachers to the disease: Violet Taylor, died on 4 November, after only a few days illness; she had been assistant mistress at the Schools for 18 years and was regarded as "an exceedingly capable teacher". Her colleague, Hilda Jeacock, died the following day; an assistant mistress for 12 years, she too was an "efficient teacher", whose loss "is greatly deplored".[49]

Obviously, the pandemic put great pressure on the medical services, not least because of the absence overseas, during the initial months of the outbreak, of approximately half of the country's doctors, who were serving with the armed forces. The *Rugby Advertiser* for 26 October reported that the majority of the town's doctors were away on active service and that "those remaining in the town are working at exceptionally high pressure". Dr W.C. Lattey, from Southam, no doubt spoke for all his colleagues when he said, in early November 1918, that: "owing to pressure of work, we poor doctors are being worked to death with the awful epidemic".[50] These pressures must have been all the greater because there was very little that doctors could effectively do to counter the disease and to ameliorate the suffering of their patients. Inevitably, some of them also fell victim. Dr Charles Ring, from Brinklow, died on 8 November. Although suffering from the illness, and presumably ignoring his own advice, he had "heroically attended to his patients until he was absolutely obliged to go to bed". Dr Ring, who had served with the armed forces for two years in France and Salonika, left a widow and three children.[51] Dr Frederick Torbitt, a widely respected physician in Nuneaton, worked tirelessly through the autumn outbreak of influenza, only to fall victim to the later outbreak in March 1919. The 45 year-old held several positions of responsibility in the area, including that of surgeon to the Warwickshire Miners' Federation.[52] Hospital nurses also suffered. A meeting of the Coventry and Warwickshire Hospital General Committee on 11 December reported on the problems caused by sickness among nursing staff, a problem noted elsewhere.[53] One victim was Nancy Shaw from Claverdon, a nurse at Guy's Cliffe VAD Hospital, who died on 1 December after a few days illness. She was 21 years old.[54]

Pressures of a different kind are reflected in the appearance before local magistrates of William Arnold, of Leicester Causeway in Coventry, who was charged with assaulting Dr David Holmes on 12 November. At the end of "a very heavy day" for Dr Holmes, Arnold appeared at the Doctor's house at about 10.30 p.m., asking him to go and see his child, whom he believed had fallen seriously ill. Indicating his extreme tiredness, Dr Holmes declined; instead, he offered some medicine and the promise to see the child first thing the following morning. Tempers became frayed, some pushing and shoving appears to have taken place and Arnold struck Holmes on the left temple, knocking him to the floor, causing a fracture of the Doctor's collar bone. The case, which was reported at length in the *Coventry Herald* for 29/30 November, may also have been influenced by the fact that Arnold was not on the Doctor's panel. "What are we insured for?" Arnold had asked; "Your child is not insured" replied the Doctor – at which point Arnold struck him. The magistrates, mindful of Arnold's obvious concern about his child's health, restricted their punishment to a fine of £1.

The Human Cost of the Pandemic

"The disease simply had its way. It came like a thief in the night and stole treasure." Such was the rather moving comment made in the Ministry of Health Report on the Pandemic of Influenza 1918-19.[55] It is certainly not difficult to find local examples of those claimed by the disease and to dwell upon some of their stories is not maudlin but merely serves to highlight the human cost of the pandemic.

Pride of place in local newspapers invariably went to victims of social prominence. In Rugby the loss of Mr W. Dickens, "A Popular Workhouse Master", was widely regretted. Mr Dickens died from pneumonia, following influenza, on 3 November, at the age of 46. A "kind and generous friend" to the old people in the Rugby Poor Law Institution, the first part of his burial service on 6 November was conducted in the Institution.[56] Even more extensive coverage in the local press was given to the death and funeral of Mr T.S. Townsend, lord of the manor at Clifton upon Dunsmore. He died on 5 December at the age of 71. For many years he had been a consulting physician, as well as a local J.P.[57] In March, 1918, Mr Townsend's son, Captain T. Townsend, had been reported missing on the Western Front, his death only being confirmed after the father's death. In Coventry, Mr Charles Davis was among those whose death was given prominence. A noted figure in local industrial affairs, Mr Davis had only just returned from London where he had received the O.B.E. He was 46 years old when he died from influenza on 31 October.[58] By contrast, the influenza victim who received the greatest attention in the *Stratford-upon-Avon Herald* was Norman Kinman, "perhaps the finest all round athlete Stratford ever possessed". A Sergeant in the British Army, winner of the M.M. and bar, he had been discharged in February 1918 after being badly gassed. He died on 5 November, at the age of 39, and a few days after his wife's death. In his prime, "there was no outdoor game or sport where he was not a most clever and skilful exponent"; his end was "inexpressibly sad".[59]

However, it is often the less widely reported stories that catch the eye. The *Rugby Advertiser* on 9 November described how Mr John Newman of Brownsover, near Rugby, lost his wife, sister-in-law and infant child to influenza within the space of three days. A week later, the newspaper was reporting that Mr Newman's four-year-old son had also died of the disease. Among the deaths recorded in the parish magazine for Fenny Compton (January 1919) was that of Francis Ward, aged 12, the organ blower in the village church: "a good boy ... carried away just as life was opening". Victims at Hampton Lucy included 8 year-old Cyril Taylor, "a bright boy", who was carried to his resting place by "a pathetic little band of school fellows". A week later, his sister, Eva, also died of the disease; she was 16 years old and had been nursing her family.[60] The same edition of the paper reported the deaths within a day of each other of two brothers, John and William Rickings, aged 30 and 28 respectively. Already tuberculosis sufferers, they now succumbed to influenza. The Burton Dassett parish magazine (January 1919) recorded the deaths of two sisters from Northend, Edith Rathbone, aged 29 years, and Florence Lowe, aged 23 years, who died within a week of each other, adding: "although they had both found homes elsewhere, we felt that they still belonged to Northend". The parish magazine for Stockton (December 1918) stated simply that "death has been very busy amongst us lately". The magazine also reported that: 'The day of the signing of the Armistice passed quietly in our village. There was too much sickness for any public celebration, most of us just felt quietly thankful."

The great majority of those who caught Spanish influenza made a full recovery, though they were best advised not to return to their normal activities too quickly. Some ignored the advice, with fatal consequences. Edward Jones, aged 44, had been in bed for five days with influenza but had then gone to the Coventry Ordnance Works to collect his wages. Feeling unwell again, he returned to bed but his condition quickly deteriorated and he died on 31 October.[61] Mr Mark Askew, "the respected landlord of the Commercial Inn in Long Itchington", died on 5 November after scarcely two days illness. He had previously been laid up with influenza for a few days prior to this but "deemed that he had thrown off the attack and was about again as usual". He left a wife and two children and it was anticipated that his "genial presence" would be greatly missed in the village.[62] Dennis Goodman, aged 12, from Clifton upon Dunsmore, died early on the morning of Sunday, 10 November. He had been ill for a week with influenza but, feeling better, he was allowed to go out on the Saturday. When he went to bed on Saturday evening, he was apparently quite well but he was taken ill during the night and died early on Sunday morning.[63] Henry Bathe, a moulder's apprentice from Rugby, insisted on playing football on 22 December, despite having been away from work for a week. Ignoring advice to the contrary, he was determined to play in a cup-tie match at Newbold on Avon. He told his team-mates: "The match must be won and I am the man to win it". Despite collapsing in the first half, he again ignored his friends' advice and played on. When he collapsed a second time, he was carried unconscious into a nearby house, where he died a few minutes later. A post-mortem showed that he was suffering from influenza, with a tendency towards bronchial pneumonia, and that his heart probably failed.[64]

One side-effect of the Spanish Influenza (as well as other influenzas) was depression and this could occasionally result in suicide or attempted suicide. Some local cases seem to bear out this tendency, although those involved were usually already depressed and the

and the hospital was "patriotically decorated". In Kineton, the wounded soldiers staying in the town helped compensate for the large number of male inhabitants who were absent. Musical and unmusical instruments were requisitioned for a parade of wounded soldiers.[10]

Not surprisingly, there were thanksgivings services at churches throughout the country. Locally, services in the afternoon were held in Leamington, Warwick, Coventry, Rugby, Stratford and Kenilworth, to be followed by fuller services in the evening. In Leamington, the Vicar had already announced on Sunday that a brief service of thanksgiving would be held in All Saints an hour after the tidings reached Leamington. When the service was held, the Church was nearly full, with the Mayor, Mayoress, Town Clerk and several members of the Corporation and borough officials present. The cross, the Union Jack and the red ensign were at the head of the procession – "a visible sign that the British Empire had triumphed through Divine grace". Another, well-attended, service was held in the evening, prior to which the "bell ringers had been at work". Again the emphasis was on the role of the Divine intervention, with Rev. C.T. McNulty assuring his congregation that the brave men of Britain and her Allies had been "working under the great C. in C. ... the Lord Jesus Christ". Those who had given their lives for King and Country would share "our thanksgiving tonight".

At noon, bells summoned Kenilworth people to an impromptu service at St John's Church. Those in attendance included nurses and patients from the Red Cross Hospital in the High Street, as well as land workers. Afterwards the bells were pealing at intervals throughout the day. At 6.30 p.m., a service was held at the Parish Church. In Coventry, there was a thanksgiving service in the Cathedral at 2 p.m., at the end of which the choir and the clergy ascended to the top of the tower, where they sang the Old Hundredth Hymn ('All People That On Earth Do Dwell'), along with the National Anthem. The three cheers that followed were taken up by the crowd below. Later, services were also held in the city's other churches, including Warwick Road and Well Street Congregational Churches, and the "lads who had made the great sacrifice" were remembered.

In Rugby, a service was held in the recreation ground at 3 p.m., which was attended by several thousand people. Just before the service, a squadron of aeroplanes, at a low altitude, came into view "through the misty atmosphere of a typical November afternoon". The crowd responded by cheering and waving flags and bunting. The service commenced with the singing of the Old Hundredth. Mr J.J. McKinnell, leader of the Council, addressed the congregation, telling them: "this is our day ... The British nation has again fought against tyranny and oppression ... and has won the day." Sympathy was expressed for those who had lost loved ones. "I think Rugby has been absolutely splendid", he said. The singing was led by the Salvation Army Band. After the service, the B.T.H. Band, followed by a large crowd, marched through the centre of the town playing patriotic and popular airs. A thanksgiving service was held at the Parish Church in the evening ("in accordance with the wishes of the Archbishop of Canterbury"). The Baptists also held an evening service.

An afternoon thanksgiving service was held at the Parish Church in Stratford. The procession to Holy Trinity included a large number of wounded soldiers. "The ancient Sword of State was carried by Lieut. R.M. Smith, but on this auspicious occasion it was sheathed, denoting that the country was at peace." The Church was packed and hundreds stood outside. In Nuneaton, services were held at the Parish Church and at the Congregational Church during the evening. At the latter, although no public notice had been given, the Church was crowded out. Here as well, the "Old One Hundredth Hymn" started the service. The Rev. W.F. Knight told those present that they had escaped from the nightmare of the last four and a half years: "God's golden sunrise had dawned." A debt was owed to the dead and for their sake he pleaded for a spirit of moderation in their joy – an orgy of drunkenness would be the equivalent of "a criminal dance on the graves of the dead". The address was followed by the singing of "Peace, perfect peace".

Celebrations continued into the evening. In Coventry, the main thoroughfares were again crowded. Some bonfires were lit, flares illuminated and at least one effigy of the Kaiser burned. At places of entertainment, the National Anthem was sung enthusiastically. However, by midnight, the city's streets were practically clear. One noticeable change had been the relaxation of wartime lighting restrictions, with "Broadgate, Hertford Street, Cross Cheaping and the Burges, all taking on a much brighter appearance". However, the country's fuel shortage did not end with the Armistice and the prohibition on lights in shop windows and advertisements remained and only half the normal street lamps were lit. Restrictions on the inside lighting of public vehicles were withdrawn but powerful headlights were not permitted. The shading of lights in factories was to remain until 20th November.

In Warwick, groups of demonstrators paraded the streets until far into the night. There was no 'mafficking'[11] but plenty of cheering, singing, shouting and whistling. "Youth made merry in the old familiar ways of youth", recorded the *Warwick Advertiser*. Some people managed to find Chinese lanterns and these were displayed on balconies and over doorways.

In Rugby, people became more exuberant as the day advanced. "The Market Place and the streets in the centre of the town were thronged with happy merry makers. Joyful sounds continued until a late hour; occasionally fireworks were discharged. A patriotic concert was given by the Salvation Army Band in the Market Place." Official notification of the modification of lighting restrictions was not received early enough for many people to arrange illuminated decorations. However, Mr Linnell's house in Clifton Road was "prettily arranged with fairy lights" and passers by were invited to contribute towards Lord Roberts' Memorial Workshop for Disabled Soldiers; more than £8 was raised. In Alcester, the streets were "gaily lighted by Chinese lanterns and other illuminations"; rockets and fireworks were let off in Leamington, "to remind 'DORA' that her reign in one respect, at all events, was at an end." (The Defence of the Realm Act had been the wartime legislation under which restrictions on lighting, among many others, had been introduced.)

In rural areas, the picture was much the same. A bonfire was lit in the evening on the Derry (the village green) at Wolston and "there was hilarity". A large bonfire was also held in the evening at Bilton Grange School, near Dunchurch, and all the masters and boys marched up to the fire with flags, singing "God Save the King". At Welford-on-Avon, following a service in the evening, an effigy of Kaiser Bill was taken around the village on a lorry, along with a torchlight procession. The effigy was guarded by Fred Gladwin, Royal Warwickshire Regiment, one of "our brave village boys", who had been wounded three times, and by C. Sabin, Royal Engineers, along with several other men home on leave. The effigy was taken on the Green and burnt. The event was brought to a close with a dance.

The signing of the Armistice coincided with the height of the Spanish 'flu (see Chapter 9) and the newspapers also carried information on the latest influenza victims. Inevitably, the disease served to limit the extent and nature of the celebrations. At Henley-in-Arden, it had been hoped to have an indoor service of thanksgiving but, "owing to the prevailing sickness, the High Bailiff advised that this should not take place. However, a short meeting was held on Tuesday in the market place, there being on the platform Dr W.E. Nelson (High Bailiff), the Rev. L.G. Schofield and Mr T.R. Perkins. Dr Nelson made a short and happily worded speech, followed by the singing of the Doxology and prayers of thanksgiving, the hymn 'Oh God our help in ages past' and the National Anthem."[12] The parish magazine for Stockton (December 1918) reported bleakly that "death has been very busy amongst us lately" and that "the day of the signing of the Armistice passed quietly in our village. There was too much sickness for any public celebration; most of us just felt quietly thankful."[13]

Celebrations continued on Tuesday, most notably in Rugby. On Monday afternoon, a meeting of the Rugby UDC had decided that there should be a grand procession through the town the next day, followed by the saluting of the Union Jack in the Recreation Ground. A small committee was set up, which must have worked hard, given the scale of the event that took place. The various institutions and groups taking part assembled at the Recreation Ground at 2 p.m. on Tuesday. As the procession moved off, it was preceded by a section of the Police Force. The Band of the Rugby School O.T.C. led the main procession, followed by Col F.F. Johnstone, the O.T.C., under Capt C.P. Evers and other officers. They were followed by a contingent of wounded soldiers from the V.A.D. hospitals, some marching, others in vans and motor cars, together with V.A.D. nurses, land girls and a considerable number of discharged soldiers (including a Crimean War veteran). Then came members of the Salvation Army, the Town Volunteer Corps, members of the UDC and other public bodies, the Headmaster and staff of Rugby School, Rugby Town Volunteer Fire Brigade, Willans' and Robinsons' Fire Brigade and the B.T.H. Band. In turn, these were followed, somewhat incongruously, by four clowns, and then by the St John's Ambulance Brigade, the Divisional Boy Scouts and a lorry full of "khaki clad lasses" from the WRAF. The rear of the contingent was completed by school children in "improvised military accoutrements, carrying flags and patriotic colours, headed by a clown as attendant-in-chief to a realistic Guy Fawkes, borne on a small box truck".

The route was lined with several thousand people. The procession wound its way through the town before returning to the Recreation Ground. A flagstaff had been erected in front of the bandstand and around this the representative bodies assembled and the military units were drawn up in line in front of it. A crowd of several thousand formed the other three sides of the square. The Salvation Army Band played 'Rule Britannia', and the Union Jack was run up the staff by Councillor W.H. Linnell, to the accompaniment of hearty cheering and the waving of flags. The School OTC then fired "rippling rounds", between which the band played a few bars of the national anthems of the Allies. The flag was saluted, with the various contingents marching past: the wounded soldiers and nurses receiving a special ovation. Cheers were given for the King and for his Majesty's Forces. During the ceremony, aeroplanes, decked with flags of the Allied States, flew over the Recreation Ground, performing stunts – to the especial delight of the "younger elements".

After the crowd had left the Ground, Lt Col Johnstone addressed the wounded soldiers, the discharged soldiers and the nurses, thanking them for what they had done for their country. In contrast with 11th November, the weather on the 12th was much brighter: "air keen and crisp and the sun shone brilliantly the whole day". The factories were still closed and Rugby's streets were again crowded with people until long after nightfall. For the first time since the lighting restrictions came into force, the clock of the Jubilee Tower was illuminated and allowed to strike the hour and a number of additional street lamps were also lit. A concert by the Rugby Male Voice Choir was held in the Market Place. Work was generally resumed on Wednesday morning and the town returned to its normal conditions. In Coventry, the holiday also continued on Tuesday, when considerable numbers congregated in the principal streets during the morning and afternoon. In Alcester, Tuesday was a partial holiday and the rejoicings continued.

Although the Armistice celebrations were understandably inhibited by a sense of loss for those who would not return, there were no doubts as to the rightness of the cause for which these men had died, at least if one goes by those opinions that were publicly expressed. In Nuneaton, *The Observer's* coverage of events appeared under the headings: "Right Smashes Might" and "The Civilised World Renounces War". The newspaper noted that: "It has taken the free peoples of the world 1,561 days to vindicate the principles for which they have fought. Victory – never doubted despite vicissitudes – is complete. The war ends with the destruction of militarism and the emancipation of a nation from a system now finally discredited." Such sentiments found ready support elsewhere. At the thanksgiving service at the town's Congregational Church, the Rev. Brooke said that the Allies had been fighting "for principles and truth", and the Rev. Masterton that Germany was fighting not only against the Allies but against God, who was "working out His purposes on the earth". In Stratford, the Rev. Hughes claimed that: "Britain had, in God's hands, saved the world." They had triumphed mainly because "their cause was the cause of Right". Nor did any doubts assail the Rev. W. Stuart Scott in Kenilworth. Preaching at Abbey Hill Congregational Church, he explained to his congregation "how a peaceful, musical people became militarised through following false philosophies. ... Development was arrested, degeneracy set in, and, blinded by years of prosperity, Germany set out on her great Kultur mission." The Kaiser, "the man with the withered hand ... his word a lie, himself a living canker and curse on the body of the Universe. ... claimed God as his ally. However, God is only on the side of truth and justice." The Rev. Scott also paid tribute to the "Christ-like sacrifice" of those who had died.

In Stratford, "one unsatisfactory feature was the jeering of German prisoners". However, this was confined to "a few thoughtless people" and the hope was expressed was that their "unsportsmanlike" action would not be repeated. This seems to have been the case – nor does anything similar appear to have taken place in the area, although the *Rugby Advertiser* reported that a few youths threw stones at a house occupied by pacifists at Lutterworth, in Leicestershire.

In general, the tone of the local Armistice celebrations was remarkably restrained, especially by comparison with scenes in London. As the day wore on, the local mood became more buoyant and celebratory but the public stopped well short of excess. In Coventry, not a single case arising from the celebrations came before the magistrates. There was a similar story in Rugby, where it was noted at the Police Court that: "there was an utter absence of regrettable incidents which so often mar occasions of national rejoicing". Similarly, Kenilworth was complimented by the UDC on the orderly manner in which the news of the Armistice was greeted: there was no "unseemly conduct" and the Police had a remarkably easy time for such an occasion; no breach of the peace was recorded in the district. The *Kenilworth Advertiser* commented: "There was no parading and shouting, just an isolated cheer here and there when the news was first broken. The feelings of the masses were too deep for 'Mafficking'. Four years of anxieties and shortages, four years of recurrent sorrow and sense of loss, four years of uphill battle against adversity and in face of times of actual defeat, had rubbed away the will to unrestrained merrymaking. Rather a feeling of solemn thanksgiving pervaded."[14] Within a few days, attention in the town was turning to the question of a war memorial, with the hope being expressed that it would be useful rather than ornamental: for example, a library or public baths. Concern was also expressed for the disabled and for the dependents of those killed.[15]

In Alcester, the rejoicings were of "a decorous and befitting manner". In Stratford, the *Herald* concluded that "the Armistice celebrations could scarcely be described as hilarious ... after such a protracted struggle, Shakespeare's town has no heart for excessive demonstrations. It remembers the fallen, the maimed and the suffering; the widows and orphans; the parents left without well-loved sons". Similarly, the *Coventry Herald* suggested that, after four terrible years, many people had simply lost the capacity for spontaneous gaiety. As the paper pointed out, "Coventry people will rejoice more deeply when their sons return". Too many of those sons would, of course, never return and the same edition that reported the Armistice celebrations also carried photographs of three local men who had been killed in action in the final stages of the war.

~

General Index